# GROWING

# YOURSELF

# BACK UP

## OTHER WORKS BY JOHN LEE

### BOOKS

*The Flying Boy: Healing the Wounded Man*
*The Flying Boy II: The Journey Continues*
*The Flying Boy Book III: Stepping into the Mystery*
*At My Father's Wedding: Reclaiming Our True Masculinity, Raising and Nurturing Healthier Sons, Coming to Terms with Our Fathers*
*Facing the Fire: Experiencing and Expressing Anger Appropriately*
*Writing from the Body: For Writers, Artists, and Dreamers Who Long to Free Their Voice*
*Sleeping in Public: A Book of Poems*

### AUDIOTAPES

*Why Men Can't Feel and the Price Women Pay*
*Saying Goodbye to Mom and Dad*
*Grieving: A Key to Healing*
*Expressing Your Anger Appropriately*
*Healing the Father-Son Wound*
*The Rhythm of Closeness: How to Have True Intimacy Without Losing Yourself*

### VIDEOTAPES

*Being Who You Are: Creating an Artful Life*
*Growing Yourself Back Up: Using Emotional Regression to Move Your Life Forward*

# GROWING

*Understanding*

# YOURSELF

*Emotional*

# BACK UP

*Regression*

J O H N   L E E

THREE RIVERS PRESS • NEW YORK

All names of clients and workshop participants have been altered to protect their privacy. Family and friends have been treated as part of the author's autobiography.

Grateful acknowledgment is made to the following for permission to reprint previously published material:

Robert Bly for "Last Night" by Antonio Machado, from *Times Alone: Selected Poems of Antonio Machado*, translated by Robert Bly (Middletown, Conn.: Wesleyan University Press, 1983). Copyright © 1983. Reprinted with the permission of Robert Bly.

Published by Three Rivers Press, New York, New York. Member of the Crown Publishing Group.

Random House, Inc. New York, Toronto, London, Sydney, Auckland
www.randomhouse.com

Three Rivers Press is a registered trademark and the Three Rivers Press colophon is a trademark of Random House, Inc.

Printed in the United States of America

Design by Lenny Henderson

Library of Congress Cataloging-in-Publication Data
Lee, John H.
    Growing yourself back up: understanding emotional regression / John
Lee. —1st ed.
    Includes bibliographical references.
    1. Emotions.   2. Regression (Psychology).   I. Title.
BF561.L44   2001
152.4—dc21                                                          00-034416

ISBN 978-0-609-80641-8

17

First Edition

*Dedicated to my loving wife and friend*

S U S A N    L E E

# ACKNOWLEDGMENTS

I'd have to write a "Cliffs Notes" version of the book to thank all the people who have made this book possible.

You wonderful people who have been coming to my lectures and workshops for years—thank you so much for your prayers and support and for loving this material.

Dr. Margaret Shanahan and Dr. Robert Moore—I never would have taken on such a task had you not encouraged me, talked to me, and even sent me the first of many important academic texts in the field of self psychology. I thank you ever so much for your confidence in my ability to take such valuable information and translate it into a language that the general public can use and that clinicians will not be embarrassed to be seen reading.

Vijay Director, Connie Burns, Karen Blicher, and all the people in the PEER™ Training Program—I can never repay your kindness or thank you enough for your valuable input and support. I hope that listening to me use the word *regression* ten million times over the last five years has not ruptured your ears.

Dr. James Maynard—I can't tell you what an excellent mentor, therapist, and guide you have been to me. There is so much in this book that would not be here were it not for your brilliance.

Robert Bly—your support, friendship, and hours and hours of listening, reading, and making valuable suggestions is worth all the tea in China. You have taught me so much both as a writer and as a man and have been generosity incarnate.

Bill Stott—tireless worker and friend, you have read everything I've written for over sixteen years—and even liked some of it. You've helped me polish my books and my life and been there for me when I could barely put one foot in front of the other.

Dan Jones—you know I wouldn't be writing this acknowledgment page, this book, or any of my previous books were it not for your seventeen years of love, friendship, and partnership. I want to thank you.

Joy Parker—my editor (hopefully you'll edit this), you've truly been a godsend and have not only done a brilliant job as midwife in this very tiring, ecstatic birthing process, but through it all you have exhibited *patience* par excellence.

Linda Loewenthal—you've been more than a writer's dream publisher. You've been a good, honest, and supportive friend, who has believed in me and my work for over a decade. I hope we both will get to relish the fact that this book is going to help a lot of people.

Susan Lee—my loving wife, your love, patience, time, energy, and support and your belief in me as a man and a writer is immeasurable. You have also contributed as editor and sounding board. Your loving friendship flows through these pages.

I also want to thank God, who made two computers crash and who never edited a line, but who at least gave me great people to share my life with. What glory comes to this book goes back to you.

# CONTENTS

I find myself for a moment in the interesting position of not knowing whether what I have to say should be regarded as something long familiar and obvious or as something entirely new and puzzling.

SIGMUND FREUD

# GROWING YOURSELF BACK UP

# INTRODUCTION

Regression is what happens to us when, emotionally, we leave the present moment. By contrast, staying present with yourself, your partner, your children, friends, colleagues, and boss means that, emotionally, you are completely in the here and now, and that a small part of you is neither wandering over the hills and valleys of your past nor trying to predict the future. While staying present is one of the greatest gifts you can give to yourself and others, it is much easier said than done.

When we regress, we go from being clear-thinking adults to talking, acting, and sometimes even looking like children who are not getting their way. We feel powerless and out of control, as if we don't have choices. We think we know what others need, but at the moment we can't say what we ourselves need. As we regress, we fall back toward an earlier time in life, usually childhood. When this happens, we very often think that others are being childish, and we might even make the fatal mistake of telling them, "I think you're regressing."

By picking up this book, you have taken the first step toward learning skills to help you avoid regression. When you understand the phenomenon of regression, you will find yourself really being seen and heard by others, and you will learn to listen to others in new ways. Cultivating this skill will move your life forward in a way that you could never have imagined.

When you regress, you slip into past ways of perceiving, feeling, and thinking that make you unable to see all of the choices available to you in the present. You probably regress because you are feeling unsafe, an experience that many of us felt as children. You might also feel as if forces greater than yourself are in control, and that you have no choice but to follow someone else's moods, whims, feelings, and directions. Another trigger for regression is feeling that someone important is abandoning you, when in fact regression is really your abandoning of your mature adult self.

In a very real sense, I have been gathering material and experiences to write this book for the last fifteen years. My first glimmering of regression came from the hundreds of workshops I led on anger. As I taught others about this very misunderstood feeling—how to recognize it, understand it, and express it in a conscious and healthy way—I realized that anger is no more negative than any other feeling, such as joy or sadness. I also knew, however, that anger has a dark cousin, rage. Rage occurs when anger festers in a person, without release, to the point where he or she regresses to a childish state and explodes or implodes.

I realized that I had to differentiate anger, which everybody feels at times and has a perfect right to express in appropriate ways, from rage, which cannot be expressed safely and harms both those on whom it is inflicted and those who inflict it. Rage is not a feeling but rather a behavior or action that a person demonstrates when they are *emotionally regressing*. They regress because they are afraid to feel their feelings of sadness, anger, hurt, loneliness, or abandonment. In other words, anger is a grown-up emotion that we feel in the present. Rage is a behavior that we exhibit when we get stuck in feelings left over from unresolved situations and relationships in the past.

When I realized this, I knew I was on to something important, and I had to find out more. Since the personal growth psychology literature contains almost nothing on emotional regression (which is not to be confused with past-life regression), I read mostly academic psychology books to see what I could learn. Most psychologists and psychiatrists, I discovered, use the word infrequently. A field called self psychology often discusses regression, though in ways that are difficult to understand. It took me several years to get clear in my mind what the self psychologists meant to say. When I did, I began using some of their ideas, reformulated in my very personal and, some say, humorous presentation style, in some of my public talks and workshops.

I went on to present this material to thousands of laypersons and professionals, and the response has been overwhelming. Two years ago when I spoke on "Better Communication Through Understanding Regression" at the Open Center, an alternative educational facility in New York City, a woman in her late seventies came up to me at the end of my talk and extended her hand. "Mr. Lee," she said, "I have been a psychiatrist for over forty years, and I have just listened to one of the most important, potentially life-changing talks I have ever heard. If the general public had access to this material, it would change the way they think about communication. Every relationship they have could be improved. It could save many couples who are doomed to misunderstanding at best and divorce at worst. It could heal parent-child relationships, friendships, and even relationships at work."

I cannot tell you how gratified I was to hear those words. Since then, hundreds of people have enthusiastically responded to my workshops and lectures on regression. Many of them say something like "John, this is one of the best explanations I have ever heard for behaviors that I never understood in myself. Why aren't more people talking about this?"

Why indeed? I've thought about why more has not been written or said on regression, and I've come to the following conclusions. One of the main reasons is that regression is so prevalent in our lives. It is such an integral part of our culture and our relationships that it is often mislabeled as many other things, such as neurosis and addiction, to name just two. One of the most important reasons why I have devoted so much time to understanding regression is that it is a universal experience, touching on many areas of our lives, including relationships with parents, children, spouses, and employers.

Another reason why emotional regression is one of the best-kept secrets in the study of emotional behavior is that behavior modification and cognitive psychotherapy are currently in vogue, which means that the cost of these treatment modalities is covered by the insurance accepted by many HMOs. The more body-centered approaches, such as my own, are often not covered, due not to lack of efficacy but to lack of understanding. Also, psychology, like many other aspects of our culture, has recently been adopting a "fast-food" approach. The rapidly growing field known as "brief therapy" is becoming popular with patients who are looking for a quick fix to their personal issues and dysfunctions.

Unfortunately many well-educated, well-intentioned Americans have been raised to believe that "the past should be left in the past" and that, at all costs, we should "let sleeping dogs lie." This is ironic, given that modern-day psychology and psychotherapy are predicated on Freud's theories, which rely on delving into one's past. Analysis involves deep exploration into one's past relationships, memories, dreams, and free associations. While many psychotherapists today have not totally abandoned this "analysis model," they have learned to cut its process short in the interest of time—with a *great* deal of motivation from managed health care.

Make no mistake—emotional regression, while it is a psychological concept, does not just happen in a therapist's office. It happens to us all the time, so often that we do not recognize it for what it is. Not a week goes by for any of us when we do not say or do something that we wish we had not said or done. Feeling "small" or "less than" someone else—regressed—is so prevalent in our culture that we have unknowingly accepted this state of being as if it were a fixture of ordinary life. An attorney named Ally McBeal in a popular television show gives us a perfect example of emotional regression. When Ally feels scared, threatened, or outclassed, she begins to shrink—literally. The worse she feels about the situation, the smaller she gets. Pretty soon she has become five inches tall and walks out of the courtroom in defeat.

But feeling small is not a normal part of daily life, and believing that it is is destructive. This is one reason why it is imperative for us to understand emotional regression. When we are not conscious of it, it usually brings about damaging behaviors, and inefficient ways of communicating and interacting with others. When we mistake regression for ordinary ways of thinking, speaking, feeling, and acting, we begin living lives of "quiet desperation" without knowing why.

Often we mistake regression for helping people, or giving them useful and important suggestions about how to solve their problems. For example, you may say to a friend in a kind voice, "I feel that you have an eating problem and that you use food to stuff your feelings. I think you ought to get some help."

Most people would think there's nothing wrong with this remark, that you are just being considerate and caring about your friend's well-being. But it is presumptuous to assume that we understand another person's motives. Who are we to say that we know for certain why our friend is overeating? Plus, this kind of statement is belittling and shaming and implies a kind of holier-than-thou attitude. The friend who hears this sentence will most likely not feel helped—she will feel small and drained. She will probably regress to some kind of childhood state where she remembers her parents telling her to eat less, or her schoolmates calling her a name such as "Fatso."

Regression is so widespread in our culture that most people are either in the process of regressing, are in the middle of a regression, or have recently come out of a regression. Regression is real. You can feel it in your body, and you can see it in your behaviors and actions. It is evident in your judgments and in your interactions with others. While emotional regression cannot be cured as if it were a virus or a neurosis, or fixed like a broken leg, it can readily be identified. And once you have the skills, you can learn how to grow yourself back up more quickly.

In this book, you will find tools, exercises, information, and insights that will help you to recognize when you are going into a regression. You will learn what to do and what not to do, what to say and what not to say, when you find yourself feeling small.

Learning to deal with regression in yourself and others is one of the most valuable skills you will ever learn. Recently, a friend phoned me and said, "You know, that regression stuff really works. My son-in-law and I got into a discussion about his running my boat into the dock. After a few minutes we both looked at each other and said, at exactly the same time, 'Do you think we should take ten minutes and grow ourselves back up so we can enjoy our fishing trip?'"

The ability to truly understand and identify emotional regression will transform, and perhaps even save, our jobs, relationships, friendships, marriages—and even our lives. While we cannot get ourselves to the place where we will "never regress again," we can learn how to recognize it, embrace it, and manage it, becoming more compassionate with others and ourselves. As I have made staying present my life's work, I have watched all of my relationships become healthier, richer, and more joyous. I have entered into the most fulfilling and happy love relationship I have ever experienced. I have freed up energies that were trapped in unresolved past experiences and used them to become more creative in my work. As I have brought all of my energies into the present, I have become more emotionally and physically healthy.

This book will show you how to deal with both your own regression and the regression of others. Once you have learned to recognize this state, you will save yourself needless pain, stress, time, and embarrassment. You will learn how to grow yourself back up and communicate from a fully adult place where no one is completely right or wrong and there are many colors other than black or white. All it will take is some time, practice, and patience.

*

# CHAPTER 1

# How Can We

# Grow Ourselves Back Up?

Several months ago a client named Gail called me to share an experience she'd had with her husband earlier that evening. "I was standing at the kitchen sink, washing the vegetables, and preparing for the night's meal," she said. "Looking out the window at the kids playing in the backyard, I felt very peaceful and that everything was fine. And then all of a sudden I *knew*, I just knew someone was watching me. I turned around, and there was my husband leaning in the kitchen doorway, looking at me. When I saw him, I said, 'What? What did I do?'

"He just looked at me and said, 'Nothing, honey. You didn't do anything. I'm just watching you wash vegetables.' For the life of me, I just couldn't believe I hadn't done something wrong, and I said, louder than I should have, '*What* is it, Charles?'

"He turned around and left, saying he was going to get a hamburger and that I could take the vegetables and throw them in the garbage. He slammed the door and I started crying. I thought I should call you."

After Gail and I talked for about fifteen minutes, a memory surfaced that she had not thought about for years. She told me that when she was a little girl and her mother and father had fought, as they often did, they would send her to spend the night with her aunt and uncle who lived next door. She remembered waking up several nights and seeing her uncle standing in the bedroom doorway, just looking at her. As far as she could remember, he never touched her or even spoke to her.

I asked Gail what she would have liked to say to her uncle those thirty years ago, if she could have said anything she wished without fear of retribution. She started sobbing, "I would have said, *'What? What are you looking at? What do you want from me?'*"

At that moment, she realized that when she had seen her husband standing in the doorway, she had briefly gone back in time. Her husband had stopped being her husband and become the uncle to whom she had never gotten to say, "What do you want?" Her husband told her off and left the house because, feeling unseen and misunderstood, he went into his own regression, back to a time in the past when someone had misunderstood his motives or had not appreciated him for who he was.

Another client, Randy, received a message on Friday that his boss wanted to see him first thing Monday morning in his office. Immediately Randy panicked, regressed, and started feeling like a kid whose mother had said, "Wait until your father gets home." Randy, who has no history of abusing alcohol, got drunk on Sunday night before his meeting and stayed out all night. He went to work unshowered and unshaven. He walked right into his boss's office and told him in no uncertain terms that he could "kiss his ass," that he didn't need this job, and that his boss "could take it and shove it where the sun doesn't shine." Several days later, Randy found out from a colleague that his boss had been going to give him a promotion. Randy said to me, "John, I felt two inches tall."

Between the ages of six and thirteen, I spent a great deal of time with my grandfather on my father's side. My granddaddy was great. He would take me on long drives and walks through the woods, and almost every day we would go to town, where he would buy me an R.C. Cola and a Moon Pie. When we returned home, I would just be glowing and basking in the love that my grandfather had given me. But then one day a funny thing happened. My dad asked me what I had been doing with my grandfather, and as soon as I told him, I saw an angry look on his face. He then said something like "Well, we all can't have it that easy. Now get out to the barn or the garden and do your chores and then get your homework done and get to bed."

Many years later, my dad and I talked about how his father had treated him. "Your grandfather worked me to the bone," he told me, "and when I didn't do what he wanted, he would sometimes whip me with plow lines. He sure as hell never took *me* on long rides or bought me much of anything." In other words, Granddad's kindness to me sent my dad back to a place in time when Granddad was just a young, impatient man trying to make a living. For this reason, until the day he died, my dad envied the wonderful, sweet interactions that Granddad and I shared.

Many of us regress when people we do not even know do very simple things that remind us of the past. In the South, where I grew up, many men have shoulders that look like they carry the weight of the world. Their bodies bend toward the floor, nonverbally communicating humility and weariness. If a man came into a room walking tall with his shoulders back and chin up, someone would inevitably whisper something like "Who is that arrogant son of a bitch?" or "Who does he think he is?" Something as simple as a proud walk is often enough to throw many people into a place of regression where they are thinking, talking, and acting as if they were kids.

Emotional regression can make fully functioning, mature adults suddenly feel and act much younger than they actually are. It is a psychological and physiological phenomenon that affects us all. Regression is the reaction we have when something happening in the present triggers a memory in our bodies about something that happened in the past. An easy formula to remember is: Mature adults respond, regressed people react. Regressed men and women tend either to overreact or underreact.

There is a word in the Hawaiian language that explains how common regression is and why it happens. That word is *unahip-ili,* which translates as "the little one in us who remembers everything." All of us carry within us—not just in our minds but also in our bodies—all of our past memories, both good and bad. When a current event triggers a past memory, it is easy to fall into a regression. Your boss calls you into his office and suddenly you are no longer forty-five, you are thirteen years old and are being called into the principal's office for throwing spitballs during English class. Your palms become sweaty, your heart beats faster, and you imagine all the horrible things that will happen to you behind that door. Probably no one's first thought has ever been that the boss wants to reward or praise him or her. Rather, most people begin speculating about what kind of trouble they might possibly be in and create a dozen worst-case scenarios.

## THE RED FLAGS OF REGRESSION

It is easier to recognize regression in others than in ourselves. How many times have we identified someone else's behavior as childish and told them they were taking things too personally or being too sensitive? And, of course, don't forget the ever-popular "Oh, grow up!"

Regression is simply unfair, because when we are regressed, we are unconsciously using present-day people and situations to come to closure about issues from our own past. A person who is unwittingly used in this fashion almost always feels angry, resentful, abandoned, and not seen. This, therefore, usually triggers their own regression.

There are many ways to recognize when you are or someone else is regressing. Before you say things you will regret, do things that may never be undone, alienate significant others, or confront a boss or an employee, you may want to learn to identify the red flags of regression. The following are the brightest red flags that I have discovered.

## RAGING AND HYSTERICS

Raging and hysterics are bright red flags of regression. Losing control is one of the most obvious behaviors. Adults do not lose control, and therefore someone who loses control is not in an adult space. When people say, "I'm sorry, I lost it," the "it" they are referring to is their adulthood.

Does this mean that adults do not feel anger or sadness? Absolutely not. It means that mature adults know how to *express*—literally, "push out"—these emotions from their bodies in safe and responsible ways.

Briefly, let me say that all the emotions we feel are acceptable and "positive." But if we *act out* certain emotions in the world, the results can be very negative. Anger that is bottled up will later escape as rage. Sadness that is bottled up will later escape as hys-

teria. Getting hysterical can take many forms. Instead of screaming or weeping, you may become verbally silent but still be so
emotionally agitated that your body begins to move in dramatic
or erratic ways. At such times, you may pace, flail your arms,
jump up and down, or throw things, including perhaps punches.
All of these behaviors are clearly those of a child, not a full-
grown adult who is trying to communicate effectively.

Rather than hitting people in the face, literally or figuratively,
we need to find ways to get these emotions out of our bodies that
do not hurt either others or ourselves. The safe way to release
anger is to do something physical: scream into a pillow, chop
wood, punch a punching bag, or kick a mattress. The safe way to
release sadness is to weep, moan, grieve, scream, punch a punching bag, or write a long letter without sending it.

## DISTORTED OR UNREAL TIME

Another sign of regression is that time becomes distorted, either
passing too quickly or seeming to drag out forever. Suppose
someone important to you says that she will call, and then she
doesn't. A week with no message from her on your machine feels
like a month. Of course, your level of distress will be in direct
proportion to the number of years of therapy you have been
through.

One time I thought that my wife, Susan, had forgotten to
write me my morning message before leaving for work. Our regular schedule was that she got up early to leave for her job, while
I slept until nine or ten. When we first got married, I asked her if
she would leave me a note by the coffee machine each morning,
just as a way to connect. After I had read it and had my solitude
and coffee, I would call her.

Susan did this every morning for over a year. Then one morning I got up and looked all over the counter for my note. I looked everywhere. No note. Finally, feeling more like a child every minute, I had the presence of mind to call a friend.

"What's wrong?" he asked, hearing the distress in my voice.

"Susan didn't leave me my morning note. This must be the first step to divorce," I whimpered. One way to tell when you or someone you know is regressing is that they get what I call the "big lip." The bottom lip puffs out and covers the top lip, just as children's do before they are about to cry.

My friend tried to tell me I had nothing to worry about, but I did not want to listen.

Finally, about two that afternoon, Susan phoned and asked me why I had not called her. I came clean and told her that I had been upset all day because she had forgotten to leave me my morning note. I knew I was being childish, but I had not wanted to call her until I was able to grow myself back up.

Susan sighed. "Oh, sweetie, don't you remember? We bought you your new laptop computer last weekend, and I told you that from now on I'd e-mail you your morning message."

I had completely forgotten. I tried to sound real grown up when I said, "Oh, yeah, now I remember. Sure, I knew that's what it was. I didn't really think no note meant divorce."

When a person regresses, his sense of time turns into what I call Child Time. When you were a child and your parents told you how many weeks it was till Christmas, that period of time seemed like forever.

You are in Child Time when you need someone or something so badly that minutes seem like hours and hours seem like weeks, or when some small event suddenly turns awfully big, or you find yourself jumping to huge conclusions, as I did when I didn't find the note. When time starts standing still, then you need to think about growing yourself back up.

## PHYSICAL SYMPTOMS

Your body provides some of the best warning signs of regression. When your stomach is in a huge knot or you are sweating like a sieve although the room isn't hot, you are likely regressing. The same is true when your hands and feet are icy or your breath is coming fast, even though you have been sitting down for the past hour.

Often we develop these physical symptoms when we are avoiding something we must do. For example, suppose you have to tell your boss that you have made a mistake that will cost the company thousands of dollars. Or you have to tell your live-in significant other that you want out of your relationship. Or you have to open the envelope that will tell you if you are HIV positive. These are all good reasons for regressing.

Even minor events can cause the physical symptoms of regression. You pick up the phone to call your parents and find that your mouth is dry and your pulse is racing. You meet an attractive stranger at a party, and your voice comes out an octave higher than usual.

Why do these things happen? These "minor" events are not really minor at all. Calling your parents reminds you of how dependent on them you used to be and, in some ways, still are. Meeting that man or woman at the party brings to mind someone from your past, perhaps a lover, who had tremendous importance to you.

A nonregressed adult has control over his or her body. Only in an extreme situation, such as when someone is threatening you with a gun, will you go weak in the knees, vomit, develop knots in your stomach, or get an extreme headache. When you feel fully adult, the thought of going over to chat with someone who catches your attention at a party does not provoke cold feet or a mouth full of cotton. You go over and take your best shot. Chances are, you will be welcomed as a new acquaintance, but if not, rejection will not kill you.

If it *does* kill you—that is, if you cannot eat or sleep for days, suffer from nausea and diarrhea, or break out in hives—this rejection probably mirrors an overwhelming rejection or *abandonment* that you experienced in the past. Your body is telling you that you have regressed to a point where you want to be taken care of, as you were in childhood.

## TALKING AND TALKING WITHOUT SAYING ANYTHING

You say to your significant other, "Honey, we've got to talk." Already, the conversation has gotten off on the wrong foot, because it has begun with the regressive word *we*. The subtext of *we* is "I have to talk and you have to listen, because if I'm going back to kindergarten, then I'm taking someone with me." If you don't remember anything else that you read in this book, remember that *regression loves company.*

With your opening words, the great debate begins. You hurl the first complaint or accusation. She retaliates with her best defensive strategy: reminding you of something you said over five years ago. You then digress for an hour and a half. Destructive sentences are like heat-seeking missiles—many miss their target but a few hit in the softest places. By the end of the night, both of you are sagging on the sofa, worn to a frazzle after a four-and-a-half-hour marathon session of regression. Finally one of you says in an exhausted voice, "What was the original point of all this?" Then you both collapse from battle fatigue, silently promising yourselves that you will never do this again.

When we are scared, anxious, nervous, tired, or tense, we are likely to regress by talking too much. For example, during a first date or a job interview, you may not feel like yourself. Afterward, or sometimes even during the experience itself, you find yourself thinking, "Why did I say that? I don't even believe it." Or, "Why did I talk about all that personal stuff? Geez, what is he"—or she—"going to think of me?"

Adults, by contrast, take their time when talking. They remember to breathe, to pause, and to figure out what is appropriate to say *before* they say it. In addition, they remember *to give the other person a chance to talk.*

Regressed people interrupt, finish other people's sentences, run on and on and on, and often say things they really should not say. If you have just met one, he'll tell you all kinds of bad things about himself, thinking that this will make the two of you "intimate." That sort of behavior is more likely to make you want to run.

Adults know they have plenty of time and do not give away their crown jewels just because someone smiles at them. Adults give a little and see if a little comes back. If it does, they share a little more and watch what happens. After a while, trust grows, and the exchange gets deeper and more confidential.

There is an old Arabic saying: "Haste is of the devil. Slowness is of God."

## Not Talking Enough

When you are nervous, you may close up like a clam, hiding behind a wall of silence. Profound silence is often a sign of regression. It is also often a symptom of psychic numbness. The philosophy "If I don't say anything, I can't be wrong" is an adult version of what young children do. It is like thinking you are hidden when you bury your face under a pillow: "If I can't see them, they can't see me." But yes, people can see you. They see the nontalker's scared, stiff face just as certainly as they can see the young child's backside sticking out from under the pillow.

"What's the matter?" people ask the nontalker. And they are lucky if all she says is "Nothing, I'm fine" or even "You know what's the matter." I was once lying peacefully on my bed watching a video with an old girlfriend. I politely and gently patted her on the knee and said, "I'm going downstairs to get something to eat. Would you like anything?"

"No!" she said in a very sharp tone of voice.

I was surprised but didn't think much of it. When I returned, you could have cut the silence with a knife. I saw how stiff her body was and asked her what was wrong.

All she said was "You know."

I didn't, but her refusal to say anything else made me start guessing. "Did I do something wrong?" I asked.

"You know what you did," she said.

I got agitated and finally said, "What did I do?"

After several more minutes of cold stares, she said, "That little knee-patting thing you did before going to the kitchen."

"Yes, and that's supposed to get me silence?"

"It means you're dismissing me."

I found out that, to her, a pat on the knee spoke volumes. But her silence was supposed to communicate a message that possibly only one other man on the planet would ever understand. After several hours of discussion, we stumbled onto the truth that her first husband, the one she had married right out of high school, was guilty of the crime I had been judged as committing. She went on to tell me that when they made love, and he finished before her, he would pat her on the knee and say, "Next time will be your turn." Then he would roll over and go to sleep. She felt dismissed, not to mention sexually frustrated.

Some people in regression go weeks without speaking to their partners. Silence may be better than ranting, raging, and being physically abusive, but it can just as surely lead to separation, distance, or even divorce.

## FEELING THAT YOU DON'T HAVE A CHOICE

If you feel you *must* do something you don't want to do, guess what? It's a bright red flag waving, telling you that you are probably in regression. Remember how often as a child you were not given the freedom to choose? Often when you regress, it is because something has caused you to feel that you are without the freedom of choice. For this reason, you cannot respond to what is happening in the moment.

But adults nearly always have options. They can choose to say or do something even if they know other people will not approve of their choice. For example, how many times have you really wanted to turn down an invitation to a family function or some silly social event? But you went anyway because you felt you could not say no because you didn't have a choice.

Often someone in a miserable marriage will tell me, "I can't break up my marriage—that's the bottom line. I don't have a choice." I might smile politely and nod because I am not responsible for that person's life or happiness, but I think to myself, *Of course you have a choice. You just can't see it through those regressed eyes.*

I was once talking about child abuse with a group of a hundred people. "There is always an alternative to hitting a child," I said.

A large man stood up and raised his hand. "John, that is simply not true," he said. He explained that he had been forced to use corporal punishment on his four-year-old son because the boy kept wandering out into the street in front of their house. "I tried every way I could think of to stop him. But no matter what I said, as soon as I turned my back, he'd be out in the street with the cars going by. Nothing worked—and I mean it. Finally, I had to take off my belt and give him a spanking. And he never went out into the street again." At this point, the man began crying. "I didn't have any other choice."

After he sat down, the room was quiet, respectful of his obvious suffering. Then I said, "I want everybody who has children to raise their hands." About two-thirds of the audience did so. "I want everybody who has physically punished their child to raise their hands." More than half the hands stayed up, including the man's. "Now I want everyone who was physically punished as a child to raise their hands." More than half the room did so.

"Now I want everybody who was never spanked or physically punished as a child to stand up." Out of the hundred people there, about a dozen stood—an unsettling fact. "Those of you standing who don't have a child, please sit down." Most of the dozen remained standing. "Now, those of you who are standing, if you have used physical punishment on your child, raise your hand." Not a hand went up.

"Now I want each of you to tell our friend whose little boy went in the street how you would have handled his situation." Each person suggested one or two ways to discipline a young child. The father had not thought of any of these options, he told us, and you could see that it pained him.

I pointed out that he felt he had no choice but to physically punish his child because he himself had come from a family that used physical punishment.

"My father didn't want to do it," the man said. "He used to say, 'I'm sorry I have to whip you,' while he was doing it."

"And I imagine he cried," I said. Adults always have a choice, I told him, but they may not realize they do because as children they did not have a wide range of behaviors modeled for them.

When this father beat his four-year-old son, he was regressing. He was punishing his child as he had been punished as a child.

## THINKING YOU KNOW BEST

Often we convince ourselves that we know what someone else needs, what is best for her, without even asking. If a bull saw this red flag, he would charge! If you think you are right about things and that everyone should do as you say, you are indulging in the grandiosity of a very young child.

In fact, no one really knows what is right for anyone other than themselves and, perhaps, their small children. One time I came home after a week on the road, tired but very glad to see my sweetheart. In bed that night, she gave me a big hug and a kiss and then rolled over to the far edge of the bed. Confused, I asked, "Why are you so far away?"

She said, "Because I know you're tired and want to rest."

I said, "Roll back over here. I'll let you know when I want to sleep."

I did not know that, having been left alone with no companionship and all the household responsibilities, she was afraid to show me how much she had missed me. She was afraid I would reject her if I knew how much she needed me. Something had happened in her past with her former husband or an earlier boyfriend, or in her childhood, that made her feel that men who go away were rejecting her, even if they came back. So in her regressed state, she tried to protect herself against my rejecting her by offering me excuses such as "You're too tired."

In my workshops, I sometimes ask how many people really know what their partners would say if the partners were not afraid of alienating them. Almost everyone raises his or her hand. I then point to four or five people and say, "You *know* what they'd say?"

"Yes, yes," they all answer, nodding their heads.

"But if they've never said it, how can you *know?* You're guessing, just the way my sweetheart 'guessed' that I didn't want to make love to her. Or you guess that your brother works too hard or that your sister should stop smoking. Maybe your brother really wants to work as much as he does, even if he tells you otherwise. And how can you know that your sister should stop smoking? You're not her. You're not God. You haven't seen her chest X rays and couldn't understand them even if you had."

I often hear people telling their friends and, even more often, their lovers, "You *really* need to go into therapy." And this is not said with a happy voice: "Oh, you're going to love it! It's such fun!" Not at all. It is said with a long face and deep concern, as if the words were "Boy, you need *help.* You're so sicko, I don't know how you make it through the day."

23

Such interventions in another person's life are presumptuous and childish. They are a sign of weakness, a hunger for the illusion of control, certainty, and importance. Why do fundamentalist Christians, Roman Catholics, Muslims, Mormons, Seventh-Day Adventists, and people of other faiths insist that people who do not join their religion will not get into heaven? Might this have something to do with the fact that these individuals are not in a fully mature adult state when they make these claims? Like most of us, they are a bit regressed in the area of religion. Why else do discussions of religion and politics get so heated? Because both topics can make infants out of most of us.

When dealing with other people, do not assume that you know what they want, let alone what they "should" want. Do not tell them what is right for them. Ask them. Do not say, "Daddy, that's enough sugar in your coffee. You know it's not good for you." Even more important, do not say, "Daddy, you don't want to put any more sugar in your coffee." Instead, say something like "Daddy, when I see you put all that sugar in your coffee, I get scared. I am concerned about your health."

When we act like adults, we tell others how we feel and ask them what they feel. We do not make statements about what they should feel, do, or say.

## MINDING OTHER PEOPLE'S BUSINESS

Here is a very common yet subtle red flag of regression. An adult knows that he has enough to do just to pay attention to his own concerns at any given moment. When a person regresses, he starts paying attention to other people's business. Indeed most of what we think is our business is none of our business.

One night after I gave a talk on regression, a woman in her

mid-fifties came up to me and said, "I think you are expressing a masculine point of view. Women are trained to be aware of what others need." I asked her to give me an example of something that concerned her husband that she thought was clearly her business. Without a moment's hesitation, she said, "My husband is in therapy, and he often forgets his appointments. If I didn't remind him each time, he would probably never remember on his own."

Then she smiled at me as if a light had just been switched on in her head. "I have become responsible for being his memory, haven't I?"

I asked her how she would feel if she didn't perform this task. "I'm afraid that he won't go to therapy. Our relationship isn't that stable right now, and if he doesn't continue with our therapist, we might not make it."

I said, "And that *is* your business."

How we *feel* about what someone does or does not do is our business, but what they are doing or refusing to do is not our business. When I say this, people almost always respond, "But what your partner, parent, or friend does *is* your business because it affects you." It's not that adults are not impacted by what their partner does. If your husband stays out late each night and does not tell you where he has been, you have every right to feel abandoned, hurt, angry, sad, and lonely. But in the strictest, most adult sense, what he is doing is none of your business.

Last year, for over a week, Tom, the husband of my friend Angela, was gone every evening until way past midnight. By the third day, his behavior had thrown Angela into a major regression. She was beginning to imagine all kinds of scenarios. Maybe he was drinking again, she thought. Perhaps there was another woman. On the third night, she followed him from his office to a large garage several miles from their home. She turned off her headlights and watched him walk into the metal building and close the door behind him. She was certain he was doing something illegal, and she became very upset and angry.

First she started crying, and then she decided to storm in and confront him. She threw open the door, scaring poor old Tom. He almost went into cardiac arrest. When he realized who it was, he was upset. He was refurbishing a 1965 Mustang convertible that he had been planning on giving Angela the next week for her birthday. She had wanted one ever since they met. The surprise was ruined. Angela was embarrassed and felt ashamed for not trusting her husband more.

Perhaps you will say that Tom should not have made her worry. But she never asked him what he was doing, because she did not want him to think she did not trust him. He did not know she was worrying because she did not tell him that she was. So Tom was minding his own business, which, as it turned out, was creating a wonderful surprise birthday gift. He was not making her worry his business, because that was her business.

Minding another person's business happens almost every day in little and large ways. In fact, most of what we think is our business simply is not. I'll give you another example. Rick's wife, Gloria, is drop-dead gorgeous. By any standard, she is one of the most beautiful women in the world. After she had their first baby, she could not get back down to her comfortable weight of 125 pounds. She was about 145. She promised Rick that she would go to the gym. When she did not, Rick almost had to put duct tape on his mouth to keep from saying something like "Honey, aren't you going to work out tonight?" He kept quiet, but he almost gave himself a hernia by doing so.

Now, every woman reading this right now is thinking one of

two thoughts: "It's none of his business" or "He has a right to remind her to go to the gym. If she doesn't lose weight, he might leave her."

The truth of the matter is that Rick was terrified of getting fat himself, so he denied himself foods that he very much enjoyed. Rick's sister is suffering from anorexia. "I guess my sister is scared of putting on a few extra pounds too," he told me. "And maybe she's afraid that if she puts on some weight, her husband may leave her, as our dad always said he would leave Mom if she ever got fat." This is a good guess.

So Gloria's extra pounds were more about Rick and his parents than about her. By regressing and making Gloria's weight his business, he did not have to delve into his own wounded place around food. If he could just get his wife to the gym, then he would not have to take responsibility for his feelings.

I have found that not minding another person's business is a hard concept to grasp, so let me give you a few more specific examples. What a child does or does not do is his parents' business. If your boy is doing poorly at school, you should do what you can to help. But if your wife is doing poorly at work and you know it, but she does not ask for your help, then it is none of your business. Again, let me repeat, how you *feel* is your business. You can feel free to say, "Honey, I'm scared that if we lose your income, I won't be able to pay the bills."

Sometimes even what our children are doing is none of our business. In fact, sometimes our reactions to their behaviors have their roots in stuff from our own childhoods. Last week I was in Chicago giving a talk. A very intelligent young man stood up and said, "I understand what you're saying about a lot of stuff not being my business, but I want to point out two things that happened recently that I believe *are* my business. I am newly married and I love my wife. She and I are now sharing the house she has lived in for the last twenty years. Our next-door neighbor, Charlie, whom my wife has known for years, is a good-looking man in his fifties. Well, he comes right into our kitchen when she's there, puts his hand into the cookie jar, and just helps himself. This drives me crazy, and I get really angry.

"I told my wife that this had to stop and that I would not tolerate Charlie's behavior. I couldn't believe how pissed off I was about it. I trust her and I know they've been friends for years, but I just couldn't tolerate it, and so I put a stop to it."

In other words, this man was minding his wife's business.

I asked him, "In your home when you were growing up, if a man stuck his hand into the cookie jar, would that be all that happened?"

The man began sobbing. "No," he said. "I was molested by a neighbor when I was very young. A week or so ago, my two little girls were over at Charlie's house. When they came home, each was carrying a dollar bill. I asked them where they had gotten the money, and they told me that Charlie had given it to them. I said they had to go with me over to his house and give the money back. They were hurt and disappointed, but he had no business giving them money. When we got there, I told Charlie to take his money back and never to do that again. I was so furious, I wanted to punch him out right there."

I asked how old he had been when the neighbor abused him.

He shook his head and said, "The same age as my girls are now."

Did Charlie have any history of child molesting, as far as he knew?

His eyes teared up. "No."

"Did your parents protect you from this molester when you were a child?" I asked.

When he said no, I asked him if he could see that, by making his girls give back the money, he was protecting them the way he wished his parents had protected him. This was a way for him to avoid feeling the pain he had not completely dealt with himself, I explained.

Now, don't get me wrong. I am not saying that he was right or wrong to make the girls give back the money. What I am trying to show is that Charlie, the cookie jar, and the two dollars were more about this man and his history than about anyone else.

## ASKING CHILDISH QUESTIONS

My therapist a couple of years ago told me this little story: A man walked up to his wife and said, "Honey, do you love me?" She stared at him lovingly and said, "My dear, what business is that of yours?" My reaction to this story—and I've seen the same reaction in many with whom I have since shared it—was one of dismay and a little anger. It took me a long time to get even one or two of the meanings contained in this story, and a long time to understand what had upset me when I first heard it.

Little by little I began to see that as an "adult," I had been asking the wrong questions about many things, walking around making huge assumptions, predictions, and foolish statements. I was still asking the same kinds of questions that a boy might ask: "How well is my lover loving me?" "How well are my mother, my father, my community, and my God loving me?" These are the questions of the regressed. The mature question obviously is

"How well am I loving?" When I began asking that question, I had to answer, "Not very well."

## UNDERSTANDING TRANCE REGRESSION

Now that we are beginning to recognize the red flags of regression, we can begin to understand the degree to which most of us have been largely unconscious of what we say, do, and live—a state of being that I call a Trance Regression. Only then can we move on to the very adult business of coming out of denial.

The word *trance* is a bit slippery, but we allude to the state to which it refers almost daily. We say things such as "He was not acting like himself" or "She was beside herself" or "I can't believe I said those things. What was I thinking at the time?" All of these expressions suggest a light form of trance.

The great French hypnotist of the eighteenth century, Anton Mesmer, first popularized this state of mind. Now, when someone does something uncharacteristic or unusual, we usually say, "He was mesmerized." One example of trance is the state we fall into during a long drive. The hours pass, and the scenery goes unseen. Where did the hours go, and where was our attention, if not on the road and on the act of driving? We were there, and yet we were not there. That's the best way I can think of to describe Trance Regression.

Since we are subjected daily to stimuli that are capable of putting us into a Trance Regression, we must fully attempt to understand the power of the subconscious as best we can. To begin to do so, we can turn to the field of neurolinguistic programming.

The best-known practitioner and teacher of NLP is Anthony

Robbins, who has taught that certain ideas, thoughts, behaviors, and statements can become "anchored" into certain neurological pathways in the brain and within the body. Suppose that when you were a small child, you heard a loud noise, immediately followed by a scream. Forty years later, you hear a loud noise, and you immediately tense up, preparing to hear that scream. Even if there is no scream, you may still perceive one. Why? Because the combination of the noise and the scream has been anchored into your body and brain.

Perhaps you have found yourself saying to your husband, "Why are you screaming at me?" He replies in a normal tone of voice, "I'm not screaming." At that moment, you feel confused because your system is registering one thing while the reality of the situation is actually something different. But because of your trance, the screaming tone of voice *is* your reality, and no one is able to convince you otherwise.

I first started coming to terms with trance in my own personal life a few years before I wrote my first book, *The Flying Boy: Healing the Wounded Man*. In that book I was able to acknowledge that whenever anyone got angry and displayed it physically, I immediately regressed and went into a trance. Whoever was angry, male or female, immediately became my father. That was because my father had "anchored" that response into my body. When faced with anger, I believed I was about to be hurt physically and that I had no choice but to receive whatever abuse was about to be thrown my way.

My sweetheart at the time, Laurel, could not understand why I became so frightened when she got angry. The six-foot-one man in front of her would shrink in direct proportion to how loud she got. Once I was in a regressed state, I would either go numb or bolt like a scared boy, running away from the father who would have killed me if I had ever really tried to run away.

Many mystics, psychologists, and philosophers have told us over the ages that we are "sleepwalking" through our lives as if in a trance. Many of these individuals have used trancelike states to help themselves attain awakening, enlightenment, or salvation. Many forms of prayer use a word, sound, or mantra that puts one into a trance. In the Christian Eastern Orthodox Jesus Prayer, for example, the person repeats the name "Jesus" over and over again. Every religious tradition has some form of meditation or recitation that induces a light or deep form of trance.

While Trance Regression has some things in common with spiritual or meditative trances, what distinguishes it from them is that Trance Regression is unconscious. Spiritual or meditative trances usually don't have negative consequences. The meditator or the person who prays is consciously and intentionally putting him- or herself into a trance state. But Trance Regression happens unknowingly—and sometimes at the worst possible time. While a meditator is still in charge, relatively speaking, a person in Trance Regression is momentarily out of control and has the potential to do limitless damage.

So the inevitable question becomes, How can we more often avoid going into Trance Regression or avoid remaining in a trance state that is no longer serving us? The answer is what I call a Conscious Regression, which will be explored in detail later in this chapter.

One of the best examples of Trance Regression is the phenomenon known as rage. Rage is not a feeling, as we have been taught, but a trance state that is often accompanied by very destructive behavior.

## RAGE AND REGRESSION

It is all right for adults to express anger appropriately, but we should avoid rage whenever possible. Unfortunately most people do not readily recognize the difference between the two.

Many of us have never seen anger expressed appropriately by a mature adult. What most of us grew up watching were regressed men and women who were silently or loudly raging in our homes, schools, offices, and even in our synagogues and churches.

This is perhaps the most important idea in this book, since people encounter rage in themselves or others virtually every day. So we will begin with some definitions. *Anger* is a feeling that every child and adult has the right to have and to express. Anger is not a "negative" emotion as many people, including clinicians, have come to believe. It isn't any more negative than sadness, grief, or hurt. It is just a feeling that comes and goes like all other feelings.

But since most people have been taught to fear anger as a negative monster, most of us have been running and hiding from their own anger and that of others all their lives. This running and hiding usually results in repressing this basic human emotion to the point where it resides in the body like toxic waste. It stays there until it finds a way to leak or pour out in the form of rage, leaving destroyed relationships in its wake.

Rage is not a feeling but an action that is taken after anger has been stuffed for too long. Finally someone says or does not say— or does or does not do—something just right, and out rushes our rage. Raging is what the regressed man or woman does in lieu of regularly releasing anger in a safe, sane way. I know rage is not a feeling, because the thousands of people I have worked with over the years have all confirmed that when they or their loved one goes into a rage, afterward they say things like "I went blank" or "I went numb" or "I blacked out." When I ask them what *they* were feeling at the time, they invariably say, "Nothing." In other words, they were unconscious—in a trance.

Sometimes rage comes out in a single explosive event. Sometimes it leaks out in the form of sarcasm, put-downs, cruel jokes, chronic lateness, or racial slurs. If you ask a person engaged in these behaviors if they are angry, they will usually respond with an "of course not" look or say something like "I was just kidding."

## EXPRESSING ANGER APPROPRIATELY

Some people have convinced themselves that they do not have any problem with anger. Over the years hundreds of clients and people in my workshops have told me that they "never get angry." What they usually mean, as becomes apparent when we examine this statement, is that they do not show their anger in any visible way.

How many times have you or someone you know said they needed to tell you how angry they were and it took them hours to do so? And how many of you sat there as they proceeded to "express their feelings" until you were completely exhausted? I have done this many times. And on occasion I have done just the opposite. As soon as someone started expressing their feelings, I would head for the door or shut myself up and leave my body until they were finished. Or I would get in there with them and bring up months or years of stuffed anger that had finally turned into rage.

Adults who are not regressing and who have not repressed their anger can usually express their feelings appropriately in five or ten minutes. When I say this at my Facing the Fire Intensives on anger, people look at me as if I had come from another planet. But expressing anger appropriately takes so little time because people are not doing one of the following eight things:

- shaming
- blaming
- demeaning
- demoralizing

- criticizing
- preaching
- teaching
- analyzing

If you are not doing one or some combination of these eight, then you just do not have much to say other than "I'm angry" or "I'm very angry." After you have told the other person how you are feeling, then as an adult, you can choose whether you wish to tell them what you are angry about and give them more details. Remember, as an adult you always have a choice.

For example, one night my wife, Susan, corrected my choice of words in front of some friends. I felt angry. But I also felt that my anger had something to do with my past and not with what Susan was doing. After I talked to a friend about it, I realized that Susan had triggered memories of the way my mother would censure my father in front of people. At such times I would feel embarrassed for him. After I grew myself back up, I told Susan about this. I explained that what she had said the night before reminded me of the condescending way my mother used to speak to my father. I said that I was angry with my father for letting himself be treated that way, and still a little angry with my mother for having done this so often.

Many people have told me that they do some combination of the eight things mentioned above. The reason is that when we try to express our anger, we regress back to a time when these behaviors were modeled for us. We observed these behaviors, filed them away, and have been imitating them ever since. When we are doing one or more of these eight things, we are not operating in the present. We are in our past, using the language we used when we were children or that someone taught us at some time in our past history.

More than a few folks have asked me, "What good does just saying 'I'm angry' do, especially if you don't explain why you're angry?" I always give them the same answer. When children express their feelings, they hope and expect to be comforted, cared for, nurtured, held, or fed. When adults express their feelings, they should have no expectations that the other person will change. Now, I am not saying that the one you are sharing your anger with will not change. But the real reason an adult tells another adult what he is feeling is to be able to say to *himself*, "Ahhh, I'm glad I got that out."

When adults express anger appropriately, they can expect to feel energized, serene, and usually closer to the other person than if they had held in their anger for fear that it would cause pain.

Most people grow up seeing and feeling that anger and pain go together. But they go together only when the angry person is regressed. When my father whipped me when I was a child, he stopped being an adult. Instead, he would regress back to when he was a child and his own father was whipping him. He was doing what was done to him as a child—thinking that he was doing the "adult" and "right" thing because "he loved me" and did not want me to grow up to become a criminal or a sociopath.

But his rage during his regression taught me to be afraid of all anger. Therefore, when people I loved got angry, I shut down and tried to shut them down. When I felt anger, I medicated it or tried to meditate it away instead of just simply feeling it.

When you sense that there is more "feeling" in your body than what the present situation or circumstance warrants, it is probably because it is triggering something from your past that has been stored in your body for a long time. As I have said before, use your body as a barometer to gauge whether you are in the past or in the present. Present anger should create very little tension or stress in the body. It doesn't feel desperate, uncontainable, or frightening. Past anger can put a knot in your stomach, make your palms sweaty, or put a lump in your throat. Past anger takes a long time to express and usually leaves you and the other person feeling depleted, depressed, and distant.

By working privately or in therapy to release as much old pent-up anger as possible, you will more often be able to keep your interactions with others in the present, even if you are feeling too needy.

## CONSCIOUS REGRESSION

What is Conscious Regression? The answer to this question forms the core of this book. No matter how much we understand regression or recognize its red flags, if we do not fully understand and practice Conscious Regression, we will have, as Emerson once said, only "asked for a new idea" but not put that idea into practice.

Conscious Regression is the process of discovering the core traumas, hurts, wounds, abandonments, slights, errors, and offenses that we have suffered throughout our lives. In Conscious Regression, we make a choice to return willingly to the time, place, and people with whom we have unfinished business—and we finish it.

What does Conscious Regression look like? It looks different with different people. First, let me tell you what it looks like in animals. The gazelle, elegant and swift, is being chased by the king of speed, the cheetah. The gazelle gives a good-hearted run and then suddenly drops to the ground and plays dead. Sometimes, because many predators will not eat something that is already dead, the cheetah becomes so confused that it leaves the gazelle lying there and goes on to more lively prey.

But the gazelle's behavior has consequences. When it stops suddenly and freezes, it has to do something to thaw out. So once it is certain it is safe, the gazelle shakes its whole body and pumps its legs as if it were running. In other words, it must complete the running cycle, first shaking to release the fear that is in its body, and then pumping to release the actions that had been frozen in time.

This is what people must do as well. They must go back to the time when they froze or acted quiet or dead and thaw out. In other words, they must act out and speak the energy that was not allowed to be expressed at that point in their lives. As Peter Levine puts it in his book *Waking the Tiger,* when a "frozen residue of energy" has not been resolved and discharged, "this residue remains trapped in the nervous system where it can wreak havoc on our spirits."

We have all been sold on the idea that people and animals have two responses to dangerous situations, fight or flight. This is simply not true. Human beings have four responses: fight, flight, primal scream, and immobility.

Conscious Regression provides the safety a person needs to reenact one or some combination of these four responses to something that was said or done to them. If we feel unsafe, like the gazelle that has been left and is no longer in any real danger, we tend to go into Trance Regression. We can attempt Conscious Regression only when we feel safe.

The first prerequisite to healing a hurt or trauma is to find a person with whom you feel absolutely safe, someone who will not shame you or hurt you further. This is not easy. There are far more people in this world with whom it is not safe to consciously regress than there are people who can be present with you, enabling you to safely look at your core issues and defenses.

What constitutes a safe person? A safe person is one who is able to give you attention, empathy, time, and touch so that you can release your tension and distress and thaw out the frozen parts of your psyche and body. This person may or may not be a professional. Many professional therapists and counselors have not thawed out themselves and thus will be frightened by your own need to unfreeze. They might even dismiss such need as being useless and irrelevant to the healing process. Few people really know how to give the kind of attention that we need to feel safe enough to go into the past and look at, feel, and express emotions in a way that is useful and not hurtful to others.

So first find a person with whom you feel safe. Only then can Conscious Regression proceed into the four possible responses to your past dangers, hurt feelings, and repressed memories. Let's look at the fight response first.

## FIGHT

So many of the men and women that I have worked with over the last two decades have either buried their "fight" in their bones or allowed it to disappear altogether from their repertoire of possible behaviors. Take Susanna, a tall, energetic, and beautiful woman in her early thirties who loves to swim and has, in the process, developed a very fit and strong body. When Susanna sees a man look at her in a "certain way," even from a distance, something in her freezes, and she becomes afraid that he will hurt her, even if it is broad daylight and he is in a car at a stoplight.

Is her fear about what really might happen in that moment? The answer is no. When men stare at her, Susanna regresses to a time in early adolescence when an uncle molested her and told her that if she fought him, it would only make it worse. His threat was most certainly real, for this uncle was a very mean and evil man. Susanna's natural inclination would have been to fight but, out of fear, she "just gave up." Now when a man looks at her in this "certain way," she is immediately seized by the fear that she will be hurt if she should fight.

How can someone like Susanna begin reclaiming her ability to fight for herself? When Susanna told me her story at one of my four-day Regression Intensives, she started to cry, dropping her head almost into her lap, like someone who has lost a battle even before it is waged. I asked her to stand up, close her eyes, and hold out her arms with her palms out. When she hesitated, I reassured her that she was completely safe and in control, and that she could stop at any moment if she wished.

Once Susanna was standing with her arms outstretched, I put my arms out and placed my palms to hers. Then I said, "Don't worry about me. Push my hands as hard as you wish, the way you would have pushed your uncle away from you every time he hurt you." She immediately began pushing, screaming and crying with the force of a very angry woman who had every right to feel her anger and express it fully. What Susanna was doing was letting out the repressed fight instinct she had been holding in her body for years. She was consciously going back to a particular place and time so that she could release the pent-up, stored anger and adrenaline that she had acquired back then. She was completing her unfinished business.

Is Susanna finished now? Absolutely not. But she has begun to reclaim her ability to fight and to feel angry. If she continues to practice feeling empowered when it comes to men and the way they look at her, she will tend to regress less and less as time goes on. As she releases these stored emotions over and over again, the fight response will become more and more available to her as a possible option for handling potentially threatening situations. She still may choose not to employ this response. But since she will be coming from an adult place in the present, she will have the ability to make that choice. Before Susanna began discharging some of her pent-up feelings, the fight response simply was not a choice for her. Her uncle took away her choice to fight. But now she is retrieving a part of herself that is rightfully hers.

When Susanna first consciously regressed back to that time with her uncle and started pushing out her anger, as we have seen, she began crying. I said, "Let the tears come, but not at the expense of your anger." As I said in my book on anger, *Facing the Fire,* many women were allowed to cry as children, but they were not supported when they expressed their anger. For that reason, when grown women feel angry, they let the water of their tears douse the fire of their anger. Many women have told me that the reason they cry is that they are sad that expressing anger was not an option—and still does not seem to be.

Only when a woman—or a man—feels safe can they begin to feel angry. As Marge Piercy says in her poem "A Just Anger," "A good anger acted upon is beautiful as lightning and swift with power."

## FLIGHT

You may be saying to yourself, "Fight—no problem. But what I couldn't do was to run away, to remove myself from verbal, physical, emotional, or spiritual abuse." If so, you are one of many people who could not fly away from the real or imagined source of their pain or discomfort. These people had to stay for a number of reasons: because they had to protect a parent or sibling whom they perceived as weaker than themselves; because of financial problems; or because someone was threatened with hurt, disappointment, or resentment if they left. Many of these people need to learn how to leave or run away, when it is appropriate to do so. At the very least, they need to realize that they now have that option, even though they did not in the past.

A person who, as a child, could not leave an abusive home tends to stay in situations, relationships, or jobs longer than is healthy. They might also do just the opposite: run or fly away from everything and everybody for fear of being hurt or being found to be inept.

Take Jack, a fine-looking man in his early forties. He is bright and well educated and looks ten years younger than his age, even with his premature gray hair. Whenever Jack is confronted with the possibility of getting close to a woman, he regresses. He has never gotten married because intimacy scares him to death. It would take a long time to explain all the intricacies of Jack's personal history, but suffice it to say that the people who were supposed to be emotionally available and physically safe—his parents—were not. So when Jack feels himself getting close to someone, he runs.

Recently, when Jack worked with me in private therapy, he told me he was tired of running—flying away. He had read my autobiography *The Flying Boy* and related to it deeply. "This is my life," he said. "I am always running away from the people I love and who love me, but it feels like I don't have a choice. It's as if I'm on automatic pilot when it comes to promises and commitments. I just can't follow through in my relationships, or even my work life."

When Jack was able to consciously regress back to his early adolescence, we found the source of his fear. At the age of eight, he had gone to work for his father, a farmer. He hated farming and he hated his father who, in Jack's words, "tried to beat farming into me." Jack couldn't get away from this harsh, overbearing man. So Jack told himself that when he got old enough, he would leave and no one would ever have that kind of power over him again. When Jack turned sixteen, he left home. He has been flying from one city to another ever since. He won't allow himself to land and put down roots.

I asked Jack to pretend his father was in the room with him now. He closed his eyes and concentrated until he could see the father of thirty years ago trying to whip him into submission. I encouraged Jack to tell his father what he had wanted to say to him when he was a boy but couldn't. Jack spent hours yelling at his dad, saying things like "I was just a kid and should have been allowed to be a kid and play." He also said that his father should stop whipping him. Jack got very angry and shed several thousand tears during the two days that we worked closely together.

Jack's healing process will take a while. He told me at the end of our last session that he needed to work on his realization that his mother was never an ally and never kept his father from abusing him. He laughed and said, "Do you think this might be why I have a little trouble trusting women?"

Adults know they have the option of leaving, running, getting the hell out of Dodge if their situation is abusive, unhealthy, or counterproductive. If you know you can leave if you need to, then you will feel safer about staying in a marriage, job, friendship, or romantic relationship.

## THE DISTRESS CRY OR PRIMAL SCREAM

Biologists have done much research around the four human responses to trauma and fear. One thing they have discovered is that all animal species have a "distress cry." When an animal perceives an impending threat, it will make a sound that lets others of its kind know it is in great danger. Danger produces great stress. Some think that the howl of a lone wolf is the distress cry it makes when it is trying to find its pack. Whales and dolphins have similar cries.

Many humans, as children, were not allowed to make this distress cry when they needed to. They were not allowed to yell or scream when they were in pain. Some were even threatened with more pain or discomfort should they draw attention to themselves by crying or screaming. "If you don't stop crying, I'll give you something to cry about" is a common threat.

In his groundbreaking book *Primal Scream*, written in the late 1960s, Arthur Janov wrote that most of us have a bloodcurdling scream buried deep within our bodies, and that much of our neurotic behavior is due to our inability to release this pent-up sound. He treated individuals and groups and created Primal Scream seminars and workshops. The participants would be taken back to primal situations or traumatic events and encouraged to scream. Thousands of people had their first "primal," as it was called, in those years.

Janov describes a primal this way: "What comes out when a person screams is a single feeling that may underlie thousands of previous experiences: 'Daddy, don't hurt me anymore!' 'Momma, I'm afraid!' . . . He screams for hundreds of shushes, ridicules, humiliations and beatings. . . . It is as though someone kept jabbing him with a small pin and he could never once yell 'ouch.'"

Some people need this screaming and crying, which has been held in for decades, as a very important form of release. Crying can be just as liberating as getting angry, running, or fighting. Many people have held in their tears for years. Numerous men have told me they haven't cried in years. Some even say they never cry.

Several years ago a man named Howard, at one of my intensives, told me that whenever someone close to him died, he would go numb and "never shed a tear." Howard is a fifty-two-year-old machinist, and like most men of his generation, he was taught that only sissies or girls cried. During his Conscious Regression, we learned that, as a little boy, Howard had been able to cry until he turned thirteen. That was the year his grandfather died quite suddenly from a heart attack. I had Howard take a few deep breaths and close his eyes and tell the workshop participants and me what he remembered. He got very quiet, his face became flushed, and he began perspiring. Finally he said, "I remember my father telling me that when we got to the funeral home, I wasn't supposed to cry because it would upset my grandmother. I walked into the funeral parlor and saw my grandmother bent over weeping, and I began crying. My father became angry with me and told me to go sit out in the car. I never cried again, except sometimes in a sad movie when I was sure no one could see me."

"What would you like to have done at your grandfather's funeral?" I asked Howard.

"I would have liked to go to my grandmother and cry with her and tell her how much I was going to miss my granddaddy. That I knew what a loss she was feeling because I was feeling it too." Almost forty years later, Howard began weeping those tears he had kept inside at the funeral.

Adults need to cry and scream occasionally out of frustration, anger, confusion, stress, or tension. Not only is crying not a sissy act, but when a man weeps, his testosterone level actually *increases*—a far cry from what we were taught as boys.

## IMMOBILITY

Most people never have the luxury of freezing or playing dead, like the gazelle I described earlier. They feel that they always have to keep moving to keep busy. "You can't hit a moving target," so the saying goes. When they do not have enough to do, or when there is too much silence or stillness, they find it very difficult to rest and relax. Indeed, the thought of a meaningless, do-nothing vacation or time off scares them to death. It causes them to regress.

Very often the people who cannot do nothing become society's workaholics. They actually feel that they have no choice but to keep working and producing. When they see a loved one, an employee, or a child who is not doing enough, they tend to regress. They become demanding because they simply do not understand being still.

Last year a woman named Cynthia came to my Regression Intensive. Cynthia looked tired and frail. The reason she had come, she said, was that her third husband had recently left her, citing his reason as her inability to stay home and just be with him without having to do anything. Doing nothing, she told me, was simply not an option for her. When she was home, she saw a thousand things to which she needed to attend. For this reason, she and her husband would always get into arguments.

"I've got to learn how to slow down and be comfortable doing nothing and to learn that stillness is not the enemy," Cynthia said with tears in her eyes. The problem was that when she became still, unwanted memories arose in her consciousness. To make them go away, she could just get moving again. If she got busy—poof! they disappeared. But so had her last three husbands.

Like most of my clients, Cynthia was intelligent enough to know what she had to do. But the very thought of becoming "immobile" frightened her so much, she would literally shake.

It turned out that she had grown up in a fundamentalist religious home where teachings like "Idle hands are the devil's workshop" were drummed into her. She was raised to believe that she must work her way to salvation, and that being slothful was a deadly sin. Little by little as we worked together, Cynthia finally began to feel safe enough to pretend her parents were in front of her and to scream, "You were wrong. Why didn't you teach me that it's okay to rest and that I don't have to work all the time?" She also screamed this question to her priest, who had reinforced her parents' teachings.

After Cynthia was finished, I asked her to lie down in the middle of the floor on some soft pillows. Her body immediately tensed up. "What do you want me to do?" she asked.

"You don't have to do anything except lie down. We're going to try something. If at any point you become too uncomfortable or something doesn't feel right, you can say stop because you are completely in control." She agreed. I had the group come in closer and form a circle around her. "On my direction I want you all to lift Cynthia up to the sky. Okay, now." The men and women lifted her up. She began sobbing deeply, lying completely immobile for what may have been the first time in her waking life. She cried for several minutes and then totally relaxed her body into the hands of these people, whom she had known only for a couple of days.

Many great poets have written about the value of slowing down to immobility. In "Ash-Wednesday," T. S. Eliot says, "Teach us to care and not to care/Teach us to sit still." Robert Bly writes in "Things to Think," " . . . Or that it's not necessary to work all the time, or that it's/Been decided that if you lie down no one will die."

The bottom line in Conscious Regression is creating a safe, supportive environment in which you can take the time to look at, feel, and remember the things that have caused you feelings of fear, anger, sadness, loneliness, abandonment, irritation, and annoyance. It is these feelings and others that throw us into Trance Regression. Most people carry feelings that have gone unexpressed in appropriate ways. Until they learn to consciously recognize these feelings, they will continue to be triggered by serious—or even seemingly insignificant—situations.

Trance Regression yields a kind or "acting out" or "acting in" that usually results in some kind of inappropriate behavior or reaction. Conscious Regression is conscious only if one's behavior is appropriate. For example, when someone comes to one of my Regression Intensives accompanied by a spouse or relative, the first thing I ask them is if they want their loved one in the room with them while they are working. If, for example, a father needs to consciously regress in order to find out why he gets so angry with his son or daughter, that person may have to leave the room. Only then will the father feel free to cry, scream, yell, curse, hit a pillow, or say whatever he should have said years ago.

I do not mean to suggest that you cannot consciously regress in the presence of those you love. But most of the time, when you consciously regress back to the original source of your discomfort or pain, the person who triggered the discomfort or pain is probably not your ideal choice of partner. That person will probably lack the objectivity needed for this process. For this reason, he or she will not be emotionally clear enough to give you the attention, empathy, time, touch, or release you need to grow yourself back up.

Let me give you an example of when it is appropriate to consciously regress with a loved one: When I need to regress about my grueling touring schedule, I can do so with Susan because it is not about her.

The more we can consciously regress into the areas of our lives that are not working for us, the less time we will have to spend in Trance Regression. If we conscientiously practice Conscious Regression, we can catch ourselves going into trance and come back to our adult selves sooner rather than later.

# Chapter 2

## The Causes of Regression

There are as many causes of regression as there are people who regress. The trigger for your regression may do nothing at all to me. A pat on the knee sent my old girlfriend hurtling back to late adolescence. The same pat on the knee may comfort you and show you that you are cared for deeply. But a number of factors greatly challenge most people's ability to stay in the present moment.

## PHYSICAL CAUSES

### Exhaustion

One of the greatest contributors to regression is being overly tired. Exhaustion has many forms. Some people become exhausted from their job. Others exhaust themselves from too much introspection, therapy, recovery, or work on a relationship that is failing. Take a moment and make a list of the kinds of things that, as we say down south, *wear you out.* Certain people you associate with, for example, may wear you down. For many, a twenty-four-hour visit to their parents' house may seem like a life sentence in purgatory. Others may be exhausted by places. I love New York City, but after two or three days, it gets on my nerves.

## STRESS

When we are stressed, we tend to regress. Stress is a great inducer not only of regression but of many illnesses as well. In the South, when someone is highly stressed, we might say something like "What is he so ill about?" or "She sure is ill tempered today." Stress makes us less tolerant of others' behavior and even of our own. Little quirks of speech or physical gestures, like tapping a pencil on a desk or making smacking noises with chewing gum, are seemingly innocent. But on a day when one is overly stressed, they are enough to send a full-grown adult back into infancy. Combining stress with exhaustion will make "a grown man cry" or a woman "feel like a child."

## HUNGER

Someone who has not eaten properly for a day or two, or a week, is on the verge of—or is already in—a full-blown regression. Hunger not only weakens the body, it weakens the mind as well. When we are hungry or have not eaten correctly for our body type, we can start thinking and acting in ways that are not normal for us. Often merely eating correctly can keep us from going over the edge into regression. The definition of a well-balanced meal might be slightly different for everyone, but low blood sugar levels will usually take a senior citizen back to kindergarten. Someone like my wife, Susan, who experiences low blood sugar can regress very easily and quickly into erratic behavior. Susan sometimes feels stress and displays signs of fatigue even when she is not very tired. But not eating right will throw her into a feeling of extreme exhaustion.

We can be hungry for other things besides food: We can be "hungry for attention," "financially starving to death," or have "a hunger for fame." All of these types of hungers are to be taken seriously, because all of them will send people into a regression if they are not addressed responsibly and maturely.

## PSYCHOLOGICAL CAUSES

### LONELINESS

For many of us, loneliness can be a real regressor. Sometimes we feel lonely even in a crowd. Although a certain amount of solitude is healthy and desirable for balance, it is definitely possible to spend too much time alone. I know a man named Ed who goes to his cabin in the woods several times a year. If he spends three or four days there, he does fine. But if he stays longer than seven days, he almost always regresses and ends up calling me.

The first thing he usually says is something like "Why am I so alone?" We talk for a few minutes, and then I ask how long he has confined himself to his quarters. He usually laughs and gets it pretty quickly that he has regressed to the little boy who got sent to his room a lot. In a strange way, when he spends too much time alone in his cabin, he becomes like the punishing father who banished him to his room. At the same time, he becomes the little boy who had no choice except to do what his father said.

I can usually get Ed laughing by saying, "Ed, have you lost your car keys again?" That is code for "Adults can't be abandoned, and you can get in your car at any time and come home."

The next day Ed always calls and thanks me. As he has become more aware of what regression is, he is getting better at allowing his adult inner time clock to tell him how long he can comfortably stay at his cabin alone.

## CRITICIZING

Most of us can handle only so much criticism before we make the great return to childhood, when our parents, priest, minister, teachers, and others criticized us "because they loved us and wanted us to be all that we could be." When people criticize us, we almost never take it positively. Instead, we feel as if we have done something wrong and are not good people. If we were good, after all, people would not be hurling such harsh critical words at us.

As adults, we are conditioned to believe that we must "take criticism," even if we didn't ask for it or solicit it. While it is often useful to request criticism of our work, behavior, or appearance, unsolicited criticism usually throws us into regression. If we are already in regression, criticism tends to intensify it.

On the other side of the equation, when we think we are giving constructive criticism, we are often just expressing our anger or hurt. In those cases, we are not criticizing in a constructive manner but are falling into a regressed state.

## SHAMING

Shaming is a very damaging behavior that can make just about anybody regress. When someone is shaming another, they may think they are appropriately expressing their feelings of anger or hurt. As John Bradshaw said in his book *On the Family,* most people are "shame bound." In other words, most of us are still carting around so much shame from childhood that whenever someone says something shaming, boom—we are right back home, where shame and criticism were like hors d'oeuvres before meals and dessert afterward.

When we are regressed, we think we deserve to be shamed. After all, haven't we done reprehensible things? On a good adult day, what we should be saying is "I will not be shamed by you or any other person."

The bottom line is that shame is never a good state in which to be. If we are shaming someone else, we are in a regression. If we are letting someone shame us, we are also in a regression. Adults don't shame other adults or their children. They communicate how they are feeling. Shaming, like criticizing, is not about feelings but about opinions and judgments.

## BLAMING

When someone says to us, "I told you so" or "It's all your fault" or "If only you had done such and such," we instantly regress. But the blamer is also in a regressed state, disguising his feelings behind the claim "But I'm only telling you how I *feel*."

Blame serves no purpose but to make people feel helpless. When we are regressed, we become like children, facing the giant Blame as if we had no choices. Adults know that "no one is to blame" for a particular situation. Adults can and should hold people and institutions accountable, but blaming doesn't get us anywhere. Blaming only demoralizes us.

## DEMEANING AND DEMORALIZING

"You were never good in school, and if you think you can do well in college, you're only kidding yourself. The best you can do when you get to college is to find yourself a good man and marry him." I'm sure that stung a few women readers, particularly those from my generation and the one before. There are thousands of ways to demean and demoralize people. We have all demoralized someone and had others demoralize us.

The *American Heritage Dictionary* defines *demeaning* as a form of undermining one's confidence or confusing someone. I'm ashamed to say that those are two of the things I used to do a lot when I regressed during a fight with a sweetheart. Even knowing I was totally in the wrong, I could completely undermine and confuse a woman by manipulating words and facts, to the point where *she* would sometimes apologize to *me*.

## PREACHING

One of the sure-fire signs of regression is deciding that another person is wrong and then preaching to them the gospel according to you. We also regress when others preach to us. When I was a young man in church on Sunday, our minister used to preach in his slow southern drawl on the various and sundry sins and iniquities a young man could get into. As he preached, I felt myself shrinking right there on the cold wooden pews. The more he spoke, the more certain I became that he could read my mind or had some kind of window into my soul. By the time he had finished his sermon, I would feel about six inches tall.

If you have ever been preached at in this manner, then you know what it can do. Many parents preach to their grown children: "Now, I'm just telling you what I think you ought to do or shouldn't have done." When adults preach to their parents, they are acting like children: "Now, Dad, you know the doctor said you shouldn't be eating so much sugar—it's bad for your health."

The interesting thing about preaching is that it includes elements of some of the things that I have mentioned so far— criticizing, shaming, blaming, demeaning, and demoralizing. Although preaching can often sound as if "it's for your own good," believe me, it's not.

## TEACHING

If you take a person who has a tendency toward the pulpit and send them to graduate school, what you get is someone who might have the tendency to "teach" you when they are regressing or when they think that you are. Teaching is subtler than the other regressors I've mentioned so far because it requires finesse and tact. Once again, at least on the surface, teaching sounds as if it's for the person's own good.

Brenda, who has attended several of my workshops in New York, now freely admits that she has tried to teach her husband Brad for five years. As a retired minister and Ph.D. psychologist, Brenda is a very brilliant person with many qualifications that would seem to make her an expert on human behavior. Her husband, who is fifteen years older than she and has a Ph.D. in physics, is no dummy, but she still tries to teach him how to feel and how to be emotionally more available. And she is constantly monitoring his progress—or lack thereof. Brenda has taken many workshops on personal growth. When she reads a book, she uses a bright yellow highlighter to underline all the passages pertinent to her husband. Then she leaves the book on his bedside table. Brad almost always refuses to read the books, which angers Brenda. She regresses and tries to slip some of the things she has learned into conversation, disguising them as just "sharing."

## ANALYZING

When a good shamer also tends to teach and criticize, you get a person who regresses by analyzing everything to death. The analyzer is almost always stuck up in his or her head trying to figure people out. Those who regress in this manner often retreat into the mind because they have so many unspoken feelings. Their fear of these feelings is so great that they retreat behind their intellect, trying to make sense out of people or situations.

The only time analyzing is not regressive behavior is when the person is being paid to analyze. Many others and I myself have benefited greatly from good professional psychoanalysis, and I highly recommend it. But when your lover, husband, or wife puts you on the couch, it is not going to be beneficial to either party. How many times have you said or heard the words "Don't analyze me"? Adults want to be talked to, not analyzed under a fine microscope, as if they were a virus or an exotic DNA combination.

When people let themselves be analyzed, they give up their own power and empower the one doing the analysis. They just get smaller and smaller and all but disappear.

When I was giving a talk in North Carolina to a large audience, I ran down the list of shaming, blaming, demeaning, demoralizing, criticizing, teaching, preaching, and analyzing before explaining each one. A woman in the back of the room raised her hand and said, "Would you mind repeating those? I didn't hear the last one."

"Out of curiosity, what did you think you heard as the last one?" I asked.

She laughed nervously. "I thought you said cannibalizing." The whole room broke into laughter.

"You know," I said, "you may have added a new one to my list, because now that I think about it, when I regressed years ago, I did have a tendency toward killing, cooking, and eating those whom I was just trying to help for their own good."

## Too Much or Too Little

If we take all of the psychological contributors that cause adults to feel small, we can put them into two categories: too much or too little.

*Too much* shaming, blaming, criticizing, and so on will cause a full-grown adult to feel small and all but disappear from view. But then, too much of just about *anything* will also do the trick. Some people will regress in the face of too much noise, too much silence, too many people, too much attention, too much alcohol, too much sex, or too much touch. Too much of anything can send people hurling back into adolescence, childhood, or infancy.

The same is true of *too little,* as in too little silence, too little touch, or too little attention. But where too little differs from too much is that never in this lifetime will you ever experience "too little" shame, blame, demeaning, demoralizing, criticizing, preaching, teaching, or analyzing from people who are not paid to teach or analyze.

My wife has a great tolerance for large numbers of people whom she doesn't know, and she will never regress at the thought of going to a big party. I need more solitude and time away from people. If I get too little silence, I will regress, just as surely as she does if she gets too much. On the other hand, it is very hard for me to get too much silence.

In other words, what shrinks you may not affect your wife, husband, lover, or friend at all. Conversely, what shrinks them may not affect you in the least. Everyone, however, has the tendency to regress over *something*. You may go through a period in your life when very little causes you to regress: You get plenty of rest and exercise, eat good healthy food, and are not financially stressed or emotionally drained. Then you may go through a period when you regress at the drop of a hat. At those times, everyone and everything seems to turn you into a little boy or girl. Like most things in life, regression is cyclical.

## OTHER CAUSES

### THINKING YOU KNOW

One of the main contributors to the regression process is thinking we know what another person needs, thinks, or feels without first asking them. This is a learned behavior, usually from childhood. Many of the grown-ups that we were around were already emotionally withdrawn, repressed, or just generally shut down to their feelings. They were afraid of rocking the family boat emotionally because they felt ill equipped to row through the stormy sea of life, especially when they were young, stressed out, overworked, or unemployed. So they developed nonverbal cues to express their emotions and needs in the subtlest of ways.

As children, many of us had to learn these signals, to pick up on the cues that Dad was angry or that Mother was hurt. We had to invest a lot of time in trying to figure out what pleased our parents, what made them happy. We had to become mind readers in order to make ourselves a little less likely to get into trouble.

But nonverbal cues are unique to each family, and as an adult, you can get into trouble when you try to apply your family code to other people. Thinking you know what someone needs or is thinking without asking them is very dysfunctional behavior and can be disastrous to a relationship. At first glance, it puts those who think they know in a superior position. In reality, they are really just regressing back to childhood, where it was in everyone's best interest to know the cues that signaled what everyone else was thinking or feeling.

What really ruins relationships is that one person will actually go for years or decades thinking that they know what the other person needs. Usually after it's too late, they find out that they were wrong.

This happened to me in my first marriage. I thought I knew what Grace wanted and needed. After all, we had known each other for years and been together as a couple for a long time. I thought she needed me to show her that I adored her. So I tried to do all the things that would communicate to her how much I cherished her. I sent her flowers regularly and bought her nice gifts. I never noticed that she looked at them and was barely moved at all. I just kept sending her what I thought she needed and wanted. In reality, I got very little joy out of giving these gifts since they were not gracefully received.

Then one day, quite by accident, I asked Grace if she would read the rough draft of the book I was working on at the time, *At My Father's Wedding*. You would have thought I had given her the keys to heaven. She glowed like a neon sign and cried tears of happiness. "You never asked my opinion on your manuscripts before. You always ask someone else like Robert or Bill. Maybe you'd let me read them, but not before they had given you their feedback. Thank you very much for respecting my opinion on your work. I love you very much at this moment."

It took me six years to realize that what Grace really wanted was for me to show respect for her intelligence and creativity and, most of all, her opinion. Her first husband had cherished and adored her as I was trying to do, but now she was at a point in her life when she needed respect and admiration. I hadn't asked her what she really wanted because I thought I knew.

## EXPECTING SOMEONE TO KNOW

Now, one could argue that Grace should have told me what she needed. But when we are regressed around the concept of *need*, as many of us are, it is difficult to know what we need, let alone ask for it. And before we ask what another person needs, we have to find out what *we* really need and want. This process has taken me years, and I'm still not as good about knowing and asking as I would like to be.

Like most people, my early family life trained me to try and know what *others* needed and felt without them telling me. To break out of that pattern, I first had to begin learning what *I* really needed. It turns out that I was actually giving Grace the things that I myself wanted at that point in life—to have someone cherish and adore me. Ironically, I never felt more respect from a woman than I did from Grace. Because, you see, she was sending me what *she herself wanted* more than anything else.

Many relationships are more "miss" than "hit" for just these reasons. Adults are able to ask other adults and their adult children what they need, want, and feel. When it comes to getting your own needs met, one of the key points is asking for what you need from those who are *capable of giving it*. Regressed men and women guess and second-guess, only to discover that they have been wrong all along.

When I was in my twenties and thirties, I used to visit my

mother and father. My dad is a man of few words, and I wanted him to sit and talk to me during those visits. I wanted and needed him to ask about my life, work, and love, or lack thereof. Instead, he would talk about the weather and the gas mileage that my car or truck was getting. Then he'd ask me if I'd like to go outside and take a look at his garden or something he would be building in the garage. I would get so frustrated and angry that he wasn't giving me what I wanted that I would refuse to accompany him. At that point, he'd excuse himself and go outside. My mother and I would talk for a while, and then I would leave.

It took me a long time to learn to ask for what I needed, and it took even longer for me to finally ask my aging father what he really needed from me.

I wrote this poem about the experience:

### A THUNDERSTORM IN MENTONE

*The wind is different tonight.*
*The leaves on the trees move easily.*

*Summer rain cleans the horses*
*grazing the wet grass in the pasture*
*across the road.*

*I saw lightning for the first time*
*in months. It looked like a ragged*
*tuning fork, and I felt the thunder*
*roll through my body.*

*Today, in a house a hundred miles*
*away I saw my father for the first*
*time in ten years.*

*He sat beside me with his bare shoulder*
*against mine as we looked at a map.*
*Years ago I would have wanted more to*
*happen and felt a disappointment,*
*but this meeting moved easily.*

*A part of me (the part that always wanted more)*
*felt cleaned. The lightning comes*
*down in straight lines and then*
*separates into its tines. A father and a son*
*and a tuning fork are like that too.*

*We talked about mileage; then*
*he showed me the peas he'd grown in his*
*garden.*
*This is the most affection I am going*
*to get, I thought.*

*Today, this amount of affection was enough.*

When I am acting like an adult, I will want to give the people I love, work with, work for, or care about what they need. I will be willing to ask them for what I need. As an adult, I will go to the people who can listen to me and ask me to do the same.

# CHAPTER 3

## FIVE THINGS THAT WILL

## GROW YOU BACK UP

We all are capable of growing ourselves back up when we need to do so. The following five things will help you to stop emotionally regressing, or at least help to bring you back to your adult state sooner: attention, empathy, time, touch, and release. They can be applied alone or, better yet, in combination.

### ATTENTION

Few of us have learned how to give ourselves and others the kind of attention that I am describing here. As I said earlier, most of us were taught that we should be helpful and fix, suggest, or remedy someone's distressing situation. Or else that we should lecture, teach, analyze, preach, criticize, and chastise. Then the person would surely be able to see their distressing situation or circumstance more clearly.

But preaching and teaching usually have exactly the opposite effect. They all belittle, embarrass, or shame the sufferer, who just needs *attention*—the kind that comes from gentle eyes or a soothing touch, or a simple nod of the head to let the sufferer know he is being heard. Attention is patient and doesn't attempt to fix anger or tears. Sometimes attention involves slow and deep breathing. Just this simple action helps the person who is regressing.

One day I was in deep grief about the loss of a very important relationship. We had been friends for over nineteen years, but we had been drifting apart for a long time. I had tried to talk the situation over with her, but it soon became clear to me that it was time to say good-bye. I was telling another friend of mine about how badly I was feeling, and he said, "You know, the same thing happened to me a few years ago, and I never got over it." He went on for twenty minutes, telling me the details of the demise of that relationship. He was determined to teach me that I could survive this loss, because he had done so himself.

In other words, I went from being the subject to the object as my friend told me his story. He meant well in his attempt to show me that he could relate to what I was going through, even before I went through it. But this kind of communicating doesn't help anybody.

What I needed at that moment was his complete attention so that I could feel heard. Not feeling heard or seen is the most common complaint from employees, lovers, children, and partners.

When a person gets attention, it often brings about a deep emotional release. Many men and women weep when they realize they have never really been seen or heard and have never received nonjudgmental, fully accepting attention in their whole lives. When a person receives this kind of attention, it increases his or her self-worth and sense of dignity and integrity, making them feel more like their adult self.

The next time your husband, wife, lover, or friend comes to

you feeling small, try giving her your full attention. If you cannot give her your full attention, be kind enough to tell her that honestly. Don't try to fake it, because she will feel it and no one will benefit. But if you can, look at her, listen, and stay with what she is saying. Encourage her to take her time. When she is finished, ask her something like "Is there anything more?"

In Arthur Miller's classic play, *Death of a Salesman*, Linda, the wife of the worn-out and used-up Willy Loman, screams at the top of her lungs, "Attention, attention must be paid to this man!" It is very difficult for a person to pay attention to him- or herself. Like touch, we really need another caring person to administer attention to us. But in order to be able to ask another person for attention, we must first actually *realize* that we need attention. Then asking for it also becomes a way of giving it to ourselves. Mary Oliver says something wonderful about attention in her poem "The Journey": "I don't know exactly what prayer is. I do know how to pay attention." I'm not sure I know what prayer is either, but I pray that someday we will all learn how to pay better attention, especially to ourselves and to those we love.

## EMPATHY

Empathy is what the tired Willy Lomans of the world, those who have all but shrunk under the weight of responsibility and decreasing self-worth, are craving. Empathy is different from sympathy. Dr. Vincent Lynch sums it up when he says, "Empathy is not the same as sympathy . . . rather empathy informs the individual as to what is needed or yearned for by the other."

Many people, even psychologists, use the two words interchangeably. The general public certainly confuses them. The *American Heritage Dictionary* defines *empathy* as "an identification with and understanding of another's situation." It defines *sympathy* as "1. Relationship or an affinity between people or things in which whatever affects one correspondingly affects the other. 2. The act or power of sharing the feelings of another."

So empathy is the ability to *understand* what somebody is going through because the empathizer has gone through similar experiences herself. Most really important experiences are universal ones. If you tell me your feelings about the divorce you are presently going through, and I am in empathy, I might nod my head up and down in a gesture that means "I understand." Sympathy, on the other hand, means that we *feel* what another person is feeling. For example, a wife comes home from work feeling angry, and she enters the study where her husband is happily humming away in front of his computer. She starts telling him about her day, and before you know it, he is *feeling* the same anger that she is feeling.

We have been taught that the person who *feels* what another person feels is a good, caring person. Many of us were taught that if we don't have sympathy, then we are selfish, unkind, or unfeeling. The truth is, feeling another person's feelings can be less than useful.

We have all seen women who *feel* their husband's pain even if he doesn't, or husbands who are carrying their wife's anger. ("He's angry enough for the both of them.") Her husband's sympathy could be the reason why a wife *doesn't* feel her anger. If he feels it for her, why should she?

Heinz Kohut, the founder of self psychology, believes empathy is the great healer. When another sensitive human being really seeks to understand us and to offer us empathy, he feels, this is the "most crucial emotional experience for human psychological survival and growth."

When I am experiencing empathy, I understand what someone feels, but his feelings are his own. When I am experiencing sympathy, I feel what he feels. If I feel someone's feelings for him, however, eventually he will come to resent me for this subtle robbery. All adults know they really should feel their own feelings. The wife will eventually want her anger back, the husband his grief. But there are two situations when sympathy is the correct response.

## WITH CHILDREN

It is right for parents to sympathize with their children. When a child is a baby, the parent hurts with the child. When a four-year-old child is sad, you're sad. But at or around the age of two, depending on the child, the separation process begins, and it should continue throughout the teen years. During this time, the parent sympathizes less and less and empathizes more and more. You show your child that your feelings are your own and that hers belong to her. You should be modeling for her how to set up boundaries and keep them in place. She will watch you to see how you distinguish the times and occasions that call for empathy as opposed to sympathy.

By the time a child is in his early teens, his parents should not be feeling what he feels. Indeed, if they are doing so, he has to behave in a distancing or rebellious way so that he can separate himself from them. They are crossing the boundary into his interior world too much. This emotional evolution is very difficult for both parent and child, but it is very necessary. If this differentiation doesn't happen, the child will grow up not knowing the difference between empathy and sympathy. Thus, when his partner needs to be respected and treated like an adult, he will treat her as a parent treats a child.

## WITH THE INFIRM AND ELDERLY

The second situation in which it is healthy to extend sympathy is toward the infirm and elderly, when they are not in charge of their faculties or are unable to think due to old age or brain damage such as Alzheimer's. Empathy alone won't allow us to protect and defend this group of people to the degree that they need and deserve to be.

It is easy to become confused about the difference between sympathy and empathy. For the purpose of our discussion, we can think of it this way. Empathy empowers another adult. It means equality. Empathy means your feelings are yours, and mine are mine, and though they may be similar, they are not the same.

Many young men and women in their twenties fail to learn the difference between sympathy and empathy. Young women are often most proud of their ability to sympathize with a young man: "Oh, I feel just as you do!" She wants him to be pleased with her sympathy, but that is exactly what makes him feel like a child. So he resents exactly the quality of which she is most proud. Their relationship will end unless the young woman overcomes all the cultural propaganda and erases sympathy as the finest of female virtues.

A woman who employs sympathy rather than empathy in her love affairs will, at thirty-five, still be baffled as to why her partners continually flee. Learning the difference between the two is a tricky matter, and it requires much more attention and time than psychologists and marriage counselors give to it.

## TIME

When a man or woman needs to grow himself or herself back up, sometimes all he or she needs is time: time to breathe in some air that is not thick with tension and fear, and time to be alone and hear the wind and rain or the common noises at the window. As the poet Wallace Stevens said, "Sometimes the truth depends on a walk around the lake."

Here is a brief exercise you might try. Recall a time when you made a decision or took an action while you were regressed. Pick something that you have regretted for years. When you think back on that event, picture yourself saying something like "You know, I need to take more time before asking for the divorce, buying the expensive house, leaving and not coming back."

When I was a boy, my father used to take me to his machine shop and show me how to accomplish a procedure, such as sharpening a lawn mower blade or turning metal on a lathe. He would show me quickly, as if the task were really very simple. "Well, you put this thing right here, and take this here and put it there. And then you turn this knob, pull down this lever, crank this thing a half turn, and there you go." I would immediately feel slow-witted and shrink down to about six inches tall. He didn't give me enough time. The worst was when he'd turn his large frame around and walk away, saying, "Now, I'll be back in a little while to see how you're doing."

When he returned, I would still be standing there with my mouth half open, wishing I could say, "Would you go over those instructions one more time, Chief?" But I was beyond saying that because I had already regressed too far. Instead, he would end up saying something like "Get out of the way, I'll do it myself." It took me decades to realize that these "simple" procedures were simple to him because he had done them a hundred times. But on my first attempt, they were very complicated.

With these kinds of experiences, it wasn't long before I stopped giving myself time to learn, to think, to speak what I felt, and to love. I also stopped giving the people I loved most the gift of time. I was always in so much of a hurry that what I was doing usually got only half done, whether it was writing a college term paper or trying to get someone to love me better, faster, or deeper than they were ready to at the time.

Luckily for my students, by the time I started teaching college, I'd learned to give them the time that I didn't give myself or my loved ones. If a student came into my office and said something like, "Mr. Lee, I just haven't had enough time to develop my ideas for this project," I'd usually say, "Look, you're pushing yourself too hard. Relax and it will come to you. Just take your time."

Nine or ten years ago, I was trying to build a fence on my farm to keep our new sheep from escaping. An old gentleman who lived down the road came by and offered to help. We began sawing wood and nailing wire to posts. Nearly every nail I tried to hit would bend or go spinning out of control, just as my impatience was beginning to do. Finally, Mr. Jackson came over to me and whispered in my ear, "Take your time, son." Well, I won't tell you how long I wept, but after I finished, I didn't bend or lose one nail building that fence.

Time is an essential ingredient in relations between partners. Sometimes you just have to give each other a little time. You might say to your partner, "You know, right now I'm feeling pretty small, so I'm going to take some time to myself" or "I'm going to take a short walk" or "I'm going to call a friend and see if I can grow myself back up." And always remember to say "I will be back" or "Even though I'm angry right now, it doesn't mean that I'm leaving or that I don't love you." These and other mature statements will usually touch your partner deeply.

## TOUCH

Touch is so important. The poet Novalis said, "We touch heaven when we lay hands on the human body." Appropriate touch can grow a person back up. Touch that is used inappropriately, or at the wrong time, can deepen the regression.

Touch is a scary issue for many people. Over my years of working with thousands of people and professionals, I have seen the damage done by inappropriate touch—and the lack of touch. I have to conclude that, at this point in our history, Americans are some of the most touch-starved and touch-phobic people who have ever lived.

You have probably heard of the studies showing that infants can exist for a long period of time without food or water but will frequently die if they are not touched. Newer studies show that touching an infant develops the myelin sheath, the fatty substance that surrounds the nerves. Failure of the myelin sheath to develop properly will prohibit the development of neurotransmitters. As a result, the immune system of someone who was seldom touched as an infant will not be as stable as that of someone who received plenty of touching and stroking on the arms, legs, hands, feet, face, and head.

Most parents know instinctively that when their infant is in distress, touching, stroking, and massaging will soothe him or her much more quickly than words. Yet somewhere in childhood, usually around adolescence, parents tend to touch their children less and less, thus sending the message that touching is somehow inappropriate.

This is unfortunate because studies show that even in adulthood, touching improves our immune system. If a victim of the AIDS virus is touched on a regular basis, his or her very important T-cell count increases.

As many scientists and preachers have known for some time, touch can and does promote healing of the body, mind, and soul. Even skeptics are beginning to be convinced of the effectiveness of the simple act of touch. As scientist and researcher Candice Perth says in her groundbreaking book, *Molecules of Emotion,* "In the case of treating mood disorders and other mental unwellness, the mainstream misses a lot by excluding touch."

In spite of all the growing research evidence attesting to the value of human touch, however, touch is—paradoxically—on the verge of becoming a cultural taboo in the United States. Psychologists and social workers, whose job it is to relieve pain and distress, are being asked on a regular basis to fill out special clauses in their insurance forms, stating that they will not touch their clients. If they do use touch in their clinical treatment of children, adolescents, and adults, they must limit their contact as much as possible, and clearly delineate how they use it. Many insurance companies are so frightened by the possibility that a practitioner will be sued for inappropriate touch that they are simply refusing to extend insurance to caregivers who use any touch at all.

This is very disheartening. The other day Todd, who had been an elementary school counselor for twenty years, was attending one of my workshops on emotional education. He was receiving credit for taking my seminar, and the school he worked for was paying for it. But he was very upset. During a break, right after a discussion about the healing effects of touch and how to implement touch in an appropriate manner, he came up to me and started to weep. When he was able to speak, he said, "I know what you're saying is true. Fifteen years ago when I was an assistant principal, if a student would fall on the playground or come to my office and tell about living in an abusive home, I would not have hesitated to put my arms around them and comfort them. I knew it was the right thing to do.

"But the other day our recreation instructor, who is a man, was seen with his hand on one of his female students who had taken a serious fall while playing volleyball. The next day he was called into the district office to discuss the incident with a group of concerned parents and school board members. He literally had to defend his action of touching a female student because someone saw him and thought he should not be doing this very common, mundane, humane behavior. Now, whenever a student hurts himself, I make sure everyone sees that I have my hands in my pockets as I bend over and ask him, 'Are you all right?'"

## INAPPROPRIATE TOUCH

It is never appropriate to touch another person, male or female, child or adult, in a certain way because you yourself would like to be touched in that way. This is what I call emotional stealing. For example, if, out of my own touch-starved need, I touch a client, a workshop participant, or even my own child, then I am not using touch appropriately. The person who is receiving my touch may not recoil, but they may feel something is wrong, even if they can't exactly put it into words. They may feel they are being robbed of something they can't see or name but can surely feel.

When I was a child, my mother, who was often very needy, would have me massage her neck or back. I sometimes felt her put her stress onto me, or suck out the energy that should have been mine.

During a recent talk about touch, a woman in the back of the auditorium began weeping. She raised her hand. "If I understand what you are saying, then I realize for the first time tonight that I have been touching my son inappropriately. My son is six years old, and his father died two weeks after he was born. I never remarried, though I have dated some. But mostly I was alone. It was just my boy and me. Lots of nights I would get so lonely and miss my husband so much, I would call my son over and ask him to hold me. And he would.

"I think what you're saying is that I should have been getting my touch needs met from another adult instead of my son. But at the time I thought nothing was wrong because he was a part of my husband and he was all I had. Now that I think about it, I used to comfort my father the same way after my mother died when I was three. He would call me into the living room and I'd sit on his lap and he'd tell me how much he missed my mother."

## OTHER PROBLEMS WITH INAPPROPRIATE TOUCH

When boys or girls, men or women, are inappropriately touched, whether the source be child abuse, a beating, incest, molestation, domestic violence, or the type of touch discussed above, they often will shut down their bodies. When that happens, they don't even know how hungry they are for touch. Therefore, they will all but exclude it from their lives. I can't count the number of people I've worked with over the years who were afraid that if someone touched them at all, it would hurt them. Last summer I was talking about touch in New York and a young, bright man with autism in his early thirties typed out the words on his computer "Touching hurts me." I told him how I had been physically abused as a child and that when I first began doing the work that I now teach, it was painful to let anyone, even a massage therapist, touch me. He typed back, "I know what you mean."

In my mid-thirties, I visited my mother after lecturing on the road for ten weeks in a row. She said, "Son, you look so tired." She began massaging my shoulders, and I started weeping. She said, "What is the matter?"

I said, "Mom, I remember rubbing your shoulders and neck a lot as a child, but I have no memory of you doing the same for me."

She let a tear fall and said, "You're probably right, son. I was always in a lot of pain when you were a child and was sick a lot. I really can't say I remember touching you very often myself, but I do remember you giving me lots of physical comfort and soothing me often."

The first time I scheduled a therapeutic massage, I was in my early thirties. Before I went, I was scared to death. As the therapist began massaging my body, I hurt so badly that I began weeping. I wondered why I had waited nearly three decades for this kind of comfort. When I was in my twenties, an old girlfriend had offered to give me a massage, and I turned her down without hesitating. At the time, she looked at me as if I were nuts.

So if you have been touched inappropriately, it takes some time to reeducate the body. Most of us should touch our partners slowly and with sensitivity so that when they are regressing, our touch won't further their regression. Let them determine how much, when, and what kind of touch is useful in helping them to grow themselves back up.

Appropriate touch is very transforming and very important. The poet Nikki Giovanni says, and rightly so, "I know that touching was and still is and always will be the true revolution."

## RELEASE

Release is perhaps the single most important of the five things that will grow you back up.

There is a Japanese tradition that is still practiced today before each New Year. People from all walks of life congregate in public places to release all the pent-up emotions of the past year by screaming and yelling at the top of their lungs. This screaming brings out emotions such as anger and grief. People contort their faces and often weep from the rush of emotions. The Japanese people are usually reserved, so why do they practice these screaming days? They believe that the New Year should be full of joy and free of stress and anger. The screaming discharges emotions that have been stored throughout the previous year, giving them a fresh start.

Japanese are angry, frustrated, and sad, just as Americans are. But they have found a way to allow every human being to release their emotions in a healthy manner. They put so much importance into these screaming matches that the person who screams the loudest wins a prize.

As a whole, Americans are not big on releasing emotions such as anger, grief, frustration, and shame. We do let loose emotionally in some areas of our lives—sporting events, parties, and parades. But mostly we consider the outward expression of emotions in everyday life to be "uncivilized," especially emotions that we perceive as negative.

Our country has a strong tradition of stoicism, especially those of us who come from an Anglo-Saxon background. The fact is, culturally most Americans are repressives and not expressives. Our need to conform (another great American tradition) prevents us from expressing what's inside us privately to our families and friends, much less to the world. Many people think that they will be perceived as weak if they show their emotions.

Ironically, we use our cultural icons to express our feelings for us. The few truly "expressive" people in our society carry the burden of releasing all of our feelings for us. We let the Dennis Rodmans of the world blow up and express our anger on the basketball court. We pay huge amounts of money to see Mike Tyson explode. We purchase movie and theater tickets to let our best actors and actresses shed our tears and scream at our worst fears. Robin Williams makes millions making us laugh and even laughs for us.

These vicarious releases give us some relief but not as much as we really need. We tend to let feelings like anger ooze out, but seldom do we let them flow out appropriately. We let our tears leak out in the darkness of a movie theater, but we have great difficulty fully feeling our experiences of loss, grief, and anger in real life.

Our other emotions, such as joy, are also subdued to a much greater degree than we realize. When was the last time you saw someone jumping for joy or singing praises outside of church? And what about laughter? When we do laugh, it seldom comes from the belly. Not laughing fully is like repressing a sneeze. We really want to let out this belly laugh, but we are afraid of the consequences. After all, what would people think? Even our yawns are restrained, in spite of the fact that yawning is the body's way of telling us we need more oxygen. It is also a great form of emotional release that most of us suppress in public.

Candice Perth takes the idea of needing to release our emotions even further when he writes, "By refusing to acknowledge the importance of emotional release as a mind-body event that has the potential to supplement or even sometimes replace talk cures and prescription pills, we're doing a great disservice." If we can't release, we can't take in all that we need to live a full life. When the body is full of unexpressed emotion, our thinking is not clear, and neither is our speech. When we clear our bodies of stored emotions, our thinking clears up as well.

We can learn a lot about release from animals. Dogs and cats stretch, yawn, purr, growl, and make all kinds of noises—they aren't afraid to let their bodies speak. Horses grazing in a pasture will eat the plants from the earth for several hours, then take a spontaneous run on that same earth, releasing pent-up energy.

Most indigenous people have daily rituals for the release of fear, anger, love, gratitude, and joy. They incorporate dance, movement, and sound into their lives because they have been taught to do so from generation to generation.

The contrast with our own "rituals" makes one sad. When I was about nine years old, I went to a Christian revival meeting. There was music and singing, but we all dutifully sat still on those hard wooden pews. Nobody moved a muscle. Suddenly, my foot started tapping loudly to the music, on the old wooden floor. The preacher looked at my foot and then at my mother, who then glared at my foot. As if I had been hit on the head with the old rugged cross, my foot came to a sudden halt. It was just one of the many lessons I learned about repressing my feelings.

Appropriate emotional and physical release can reduce all the things that cause people to regress. It reduces tension, stress, and tightness in the muscles. We can finally relax and take a deep breath. We can get on with being adults.

Some people know they need to release but are afraid of what others might think or feel about them if they were to do so. This is the type of person who, when they are dying, see someone else's life flashing before their eyes.

During a break in one of my workshops, a woman said to me, "The technique you mention in your book *Facing the Fire,* about being in your car and rolling up all the windows and screaming out any daily frustrations from work before going home, isn't quite working for me."

"Really, why not?" I asked, curious. This technique has proven to be quite effective for many people.

"When I'm driving, it works fine. But when I come to a stop sign or light, I have to stop."

"Why do you have to stop? Is it damaging to your vocal cords?" I asked.

"No," she answered back, annoyed at my lack of understanding. "It's because of the other people at the stop sign or the red light. When they see me scream and carry on like that, what must they be thinking of me?"

"Who are those people?" I asked.

She looked disgusted. "Well, I don't know *who* those people are."

"Then why do you care about what they think?"

As many of us were, this woman had been taught to put other people's thoughts, feelings, wants, and needs before her own. If we don't put others first, we are labeled "selfish." But taking care of yourself is not selfish, and taking care of people for whom you are not responsible is unhealthy.

Crying, yelling, and screaming are all appropriate ways to release our feelings, but release comes in many different shapes and forms. Some of the other healthy ways of releasing emotions are:

- Laughing
- Pushing
- Pounding
- Tearing
- Stomping
- Breaking
- Pulling
- Yawning
- Throwing
- Coughing
- Twisting
- Running
- Breathing

It is not appropriate to release your emotions *at* people. But people who make you feel safe can be present and can even help to facilitate the process. In fact, having someone hold the space during the process of emotional release is one of the most effective ways to let go of stored feelings. That is why I have created most of my workshops around facilitating emotional release. Once our emotions are released, we can then integrate new and useful information, ideas, and insights that can change us forever for the better.

All of these methods of release can be positive and constructive if done in appropriate places, at appropriate times. Different forms of release will work differently for different people depending upon their body type and personality. Use the kind of release that is most appropriate for you. A client who was very meek, mild, and introspective would take tissues from the box and rip each one in half when she was angry. This worked for her. Another client would go to yard sales, buy cheap dishes, and periodically take them into his backyard or garage and throw them up against the wall. He reveled in the release in hearing the sound of all those breaking plates.

Talking can also be a major form of release, as long as it is highly animated and energetic. Unfortunately, few people can talk out the anger of having been beaten, the grief of having been abandoned, or the frustration of getting fired from a long-term job. To release those feelings, most people need movement and sound to accompany their talking.

The first step in emotional release is to give yourself permission to do it. Accept that doing it is not only okay but necessary for your physical, spiritual, and emotional health.

The term "going postal" was coined after a series of post office shootings that occurred across the nation a few years back. The gunmen who lost control were repressives, not unlike most of us. They would not allow themselves to let go—until one day they exploded. That can be one of the extreme consequences of stuffing your feelings and not releasing them. Other consequences include illness, passive-aggressive behavior, codependency, addiction, rage, violence, depression, and unhappiness.

Until you are comfortable releasing your own anger, sadness, fear, love, and joy, you probably will not be comfortable being with others who can release their feelings freely and easily. As soon as someone lets a teardrop fall, you may be the person who must pat him on the back and say, "There, there, it will be all right" or "Don't be sad." These statements are meant to be comforting, but actually they encourage denial of the feeling itself. If you are a therapist, you might truly hurt your angry client by saying something like, "You're not really angry. Let's go for what's underneath. Anger is usually just covering up another emotion." Therapists who say this usually have not yet learned that anger is just a feeling and probably cannot readily and comfortably express their own feelings.

Most children come into this world crying, stomping, and screaming. They throw their toys and pound their fists into little pillows, and they laugh out loud for no particular reason until some regressed grown-up tells them to stop. This behavior is not acceptable, they are warned, and it's not nice. So they shut their little bodies down and become good little repressives. When they grow up, they become silent or raging alcoholics, drug addicts, or work addicts, frigid or nonorgasmic civilized adults who must seek therapy or treatment.

They might find an expressive partner who will do the work of expressing their emotions for them. People who cannot express their feelings are often unconsciously drawn to people who express "enough anger for the both of them." People who are not readily able to express sadness or grief will be drawn to people who can carry their sadness as well as their own. In my family, my father was "angry enough for all of us" and was the only one allowed to express anger. My mother was "sad enough for everyone," including my father, who seldom shed a tear. I became silently angry and very depressed trying not to be like either parent—either the angry one or the sad one.

It is essential that we become skilled at these five things that, when we regress, will grow us back up. Some of them, such as attention, empathy, and touch, require the presence of another person. Time and release can be done either alone or in the company of safe people. Becoming part of a conscious community of people who are committed to staying adults as much as possible and who are safe to be around when they regress will improve all your relationships. This community might include your friends and family, but it might also include a competent therapist and an ongoing support group that can provide empathy, touch, attention, and release.

# C H A P T E R     4

## FAMILY: GROUND ZERO FOR REGRESSION

Adults need to let go of their children, to stop parenting them, but when is the right time to do so? Child psychologists seem to agree that separation is a developmental process that begins when the child is around the age of two. Little by little, the parent gives the child more and more autonomy. When we don't let go of our children or allow them to be adults, we are regressing, playing out patterns from our own childhood or getting stuck in issues that we ourselves need to resolve.

Letting go is difficult for many of us who are parents because we have been taught that "your children will always be your children." I have heard countless men and women refer to their forty-year-old son or daughter as their "baby."

Once I was giving a five-day seminar at the Omega Institute. On the third day during a break, a man in his mid-sixties, six feet tall with hands as big as skillets, came up to me. He looked tired and rather depressed. "I need to ask you a question about letting go of your children." Tears welled up in his eyes. "My boy keeps getting into trouble, and I don't know what to do. He's a good boy and I love him. I have put him through three rehabs now, and it doesn't seem to be helping him at all. Me and his mother are about broke."

I interrupted him to say, "Before you go any further, let me ask you, how old is your 'boy'?"

"He'll be thirty-six his next birthday."

I looked at the man kindly and asked, "Is it possible that when your son really *was* a boy, you weren't there for him?" He had spoken earlier in the workshop about not being around much when his son was growing up, and having had a father who had been the same way. I went on, "Now, out of guilt because you were not there for him, you are treating him like a little boy by bailing him out of his very adult problems. I applaud any parent who will step up and help their adult children with problems or pain, but three rehabs sounds like something other than *being there* for your children."

By now he was sobbing deeply. "You're right. I should have been a better father when he was little. I wasn't there, and I thought I could make it up to him by sending him to rehab. He's in jail now for stealing to support his habit, and I've been wondering what I can sell to bail him out. Maybe I should just let him grow up. Maybe that's the best thing I could give him—allowing him to clean up his own messes."

Adult "children" commonly regress, for their part, by being unable to let go of their mother or father. When is it time for adult children to stop *sonning* or *daughtering* their parents? These are terms that I have coined to describe adult children who continue to act like a son or daughter well into their twenties, thirties, forties, fifties, sixties, and yes, even seventies.

A good illustration of *sonning* is the thirty-six-year-old man who went through three rehabs: He is still acting like a *boy* instead of an adult. Many women also *daughter* their parents, like

Evelyn, the owner of a chain of computer stores. When Evelyn decides to take a day off from work, she instructs her employees to tell her mother, should she call, that she is away in one of the other stores. Evelyn maintains that her parents are proud of her, but she admits that "if they knew I took days off when I wasn't sick, they'd be very disappointed in me, so I don't want them to find out."

"Who else do you have your employees lie to about your whereabouts?" I asked Evelyn.

She looked at me as if I were crazy. "No one. I'm my own boss," she said.

As I write this, Christmas is in the air. Carolers stroll by the house, the Salvation Army is ringing its bells, malls are overflowing, and Internet shopping is going stronger than ever. This is the season not only for giving but for getting depressed and regressed.

My friends Barbara and Bill are newlyweds in their early thirties—this is the first marriage for both of them. They bought a new home in the suburbs of Chicago, where Bill works as an accountant and Barbara is a counselor in an adolescent treatment center. For their first Christmas in their new home, they invited Bill's parents to come over. This was a break in tradition for Bill, since he usually spent the holiday at his parents' home in West Virginia. Barbara told me that before his parents arrived she was a little anxious about how this break with tradition was going to go for her and Bill.

As it turns out, the break wasn't very big. When Bill's parents arrived, they unloaded the boxes of ornaments and Christmas decorations that they always put up in their own home. Bill's father said hello and, as Barbara described it, "took over the show." Over the next three days, Bill sat back and watched his new home being transformed into his parents' home. Barbara told me that she didn't object because she thought this was what Bill wanted, since he didn't seem to be disturbed or upset. "We ended up doing Christmas just as if we were at their house," she said.

After the holiday, his family boxed up everything, loaded the van, and said their good-byes. Barbara turned to Bill and asked, "So, did you enjoy your Christmas with your folks?"

"God no," he said. "It was terrible. I can't believe they took over everything."

Barbara was shocked. "I thought you were happy and that you wanted them to do what they did. You didn't stop them."

"*Me* stop my *dad*? You know my father. When he gets something in his mind, there's no turning back."

Barbara, who had not had the Christmas that she wanted either, went into a regression. She screamed at Bill, "You big baby! I can't believe you let your parents walk all over you! I put up with three days of this because I thought it would make you happy!"

Bill, Barbara, and Bill's parents were all regressed that Christmas. They all took a journey back to *the way it's always been.*

Speaking of the holidays, how many of you have wanted, at one time or another, to say to your parents, "I am [or we are] not coming home for Christmas this year. We are going to Hawaii [or the Caribbean]. Merry Christmas to all, and to all a good-bye."

But you didn't. You dutifully fulfilled your obligations and went when you really didn't want to go. But you really were not all there. Some part of you was walking the beaches and star gazing at night, or your head was in the Caribbean clouds.

Within the family, things are said and done that wouldn't be said or done in any other context or relationship. Every time

Saul goes home, he has the same lackluster conversation with his father. Saul is thirty-two and in graduate school. He is very bright, but he is uncertain about his future. He is still trying to find his place in the world. Whenever Saul visits his parents, his father asks him, "When are you going to grow up and get a real job? It's time to put down roots and raise a family and stop acting like a kid." According to Saul, this remark is the beginning of the end of any meaningful conversation with his dad. He usually leaves his father's house angry and vowing to never go back.

I asked Saul a simple question at the anger workshop he attended: "Who else would you let talk to you this way?"

Without a moment's hesitation, Saul answered, "No one."

"Then why do you let your father talk to you like this?"

"What can I do? He's my dad. We've always fought about my lack of direction, ever since I was in junior high."

"Maybe it's time to leave junior high," I said. "If I remember correctly it wasn't that much fun."

When I was in my thirties, if I stayed with my folks for too long, I used to regress so fast that my voice would get squeaky. I'd get so small, I wouldn't be able to see over the steering wheel of my car to drive back home. Back then my dad, my mom, and I would all time-travel back to the 1950s. One time I was watching television with my parents, my brother, and my sister. At precisely ten o'clock, my dad announced, "Well, it's time to go to bed." And we all got up and went to our bedrooms.

As I was turning out the light, it hit me. "Damn, I'm thirty years old, and I just got told to go to bed, and I did." Ten o'clock had been our bedtime as children, so when my father told us to go to bed, our brains just went into automatic parent pilot. This is a true story!

Understanding regression intellectually is one thing, but

walking the walk is quite another. The last time my wife and I visited my parents, my mother said good-naturedly, "All right, everyone go wash their hands before dinner." I washed my hands, thanks to yet another automatic parent pilot program, but my wife went into her own regression and rebelled.

Apart from your parents, no one else knows more about your early history than your siblings. Regression is common among brothers and sisters because few of us really know our brothers and sisters, or are known by them, as adults. So when we get around each other, we tend to automatically fall back into the old behaviors and roles we assumed when we were children playing in the backyard, the living room, the barn, the doll house, the treehouse, or on the street corner. They remember how you were, and you remember how they were. They had little names that only they called us, and we had some pretty good names for them too. "Little Sister" and "Little Bit" were some of the nicer ones I called my sister.

My sister is now in her forties, and my brother is in his late thirties. Both of them are very thoughtful, intelligent adults. Yet I still have a tendency to think of them as "little." My tendency to patronize them, give them advice, or try to fix them has not been met with much enthusiasm, because they need to be treated as the adults they truly are.

Recently a friend returned from his annual Christmas visit "to hell," as he calls it. Robert told me, "Everything is pretty much like it was when I was a kid. My big brother Earl picked on me from the moment I got there until the moment I left. My father barked out commands to us all, and my mother worked her fingers to the bone and then complained that no one really appreciated all her untiring efforts to make it a good holiday for us all. I swear, I don't know why we put ourselves through such an ordeal."

Now, don't get me wrong. I'm not trying to push your buttons or advocate an Ebenezer Scrooge routine. The holidays and visits home in general can be wonderful, and I look forward to them more with each passing year. But to truly enjoy the time we spend with parents and siblings, it is important to try to stay in an adult place with them.

One of the best things you can do in any situation, especially a family function, is to remember to breathe. Regression and shallow breathing are connected, so full deep breathing can minimize regression. I waited until this point in the chapter to bring up this very simple idea because everyone has heard it ad nauseam. Even as children we heard, "Now take a few deep breaths and try to calm down." The other most common advice we hear regarding breathing is "Take a deep breath and count to ten before saying anything."

Deep breathing is a very important form of communication. It is your body's way of saying, "I'm okay. I'm still here, I'm listening, and I'm not too afraid." Conversely, if you take shallow breaths, or almost entirely stop breathing, then your body will speak louder than any words of comfort that you may be speaking to someone. Your body will be sending them the nonverbal message that you are going into a Trance Regression and that you want them to stop what they are doing as soon as possible.

Full deep breathing automatically helps you to stay expanded. Shallow breathing promotes contraction. Not only does it constrict the blood flow around your heart, but it also minimizes the blood that feeds your brain. Therefore your thinking will not be as clear.

A number of books have been written about breathing, so I will not belabor the point here. Suffice it to say that when you are scared, regressed, or threatened, you tend to forget to breathe, which further perpetuates your regression. If you are talking to someone who is breathing only shallow breaths, you will soon entrain your breathing with theirs, and you will both be headed for childhood.

## EVERY GROWN-UP IS SOMEONE'S SON OR DAUGHTER

Parents hold a great deal of power over their children, and some try to keep that power even when the children are supposedly grown-ups and may even have children of their own. I remember that as soon as my mother walked through my grandmother's door, she turned into a child. My grandmother treated her like a child, and my mother let her. As a boy, it was very confusing for me to watch my powerful mother turn back into a small daughter who dared not defy her mother's wishes and wants.

In other cases, parents tire of parenting their adult children and wish their adult children would stop looking to them to be parents. They want their kids to grow up and become equals—and maybe even friends. Many of these parents don't know how to say they want to be released from parenting, for fear of losing their children's affections. I have heard hundreds of men and women say they want to get on with their lives and move into some other stage of relationship with their adult children.

My mother told me that before her mother died, she had a heart-to-heart talk with her. For the first time, my mother felt like she was being treated as an adult and that her mother acted more like an adult. By remembering that everyone is someone's son or daughter, we might be able to cut each other a little more slack when we see each other regress, especially around parents.

When we realize just how much this biological relationship is still affecting so many of our present and past relationships, we can also be a little gentler with ourselves and others.

The ties you share with your mother and father can be seen very clearly when you meet someone new and quickly feel a kinship in spirit with them. "She already knows me, and I feel like I know her," you may say. In California these sorts of new acquaintances are referred to as soul mates because *something* about them feels familiar. The lover feels already known and understood by this "perfect" stranger.

If you go to the dictionary and look up the word *familiar,* you will find the word *family.* When someone feels familiar to you so soon into the relationship, it is probably because he or she has certain traits, habits, quirks, or idiosyncrasies that remind you (usually for the good at first) of something you feel around your family. It could be anything—the way the new acquaintance smiles, stands, sits, laughs, or makes jokes. It could be just a look in their eyes or the way they smell—and whoosh, you're right back home again.

The romantic plane isn't the only place where we find replacement parents. You may have had a boss who is almost exactly like one of your parents, an older sibling, or an ex-wife or husband. Why we relate to people in this manner, no one can say for sure. But I believe the psyche scans the environment for patterns of behavior that are familiar and comfortable, even if these patterns are unhealthy ones. Why? Because for most of us, the familiar reduces anxiety about the unknown. We can rest a little easier when we know what to expect from people.

In the past, my own tendency was always to look for a woman who reminded me of my mother—who had both her good and bad points. For years I could usually find some woman who would unconsciously play that role—until we came to a point in the relationship where either she or I realized what we were doing.

Looking exclusively for the familiar is regressive behavior. As adults, when we move toward the unknown and are able to keep our responses more often in the present, we learn to manage the anxiety of not knowing what is going to happen next. Adults can handle this uncertainty. Children, usually out of necessity, need some predictability in their lives in order to create the illusion of security.

One of the greatest illusions that many adults share is the belief that if we just wish hard enough, a great mother or father will appear to take care of us, should we not be able to take care of ourselves sufficiently. When we continue to try to be children to our parents and win their approval or affection, we do so in the hopes that someday they will parent us in the way we wish we had been parented. This behavior can go on for ten, twenty, or even fifty years.

## SAYING GOOD-BYE TO MOM AND DAD

One of the best ways to reduce the amount of time you spend in regression is to practice the very difficult process of saying good-bye to Mom and Dad. I am not, in any way, suggesting that you never see or talk to your parents again. What I am proposing, as a tool to minimize regression, is that you consciously go back in time and discover who these people really were and who they were not. You need to feel all the old feelings associated with your *ghost parents.*

Ghost parents are the parents that we had or thought we had as children but who no longer exist now that we are grown. Time did not stand still for your parents. They moved on with their lives and their personal development, just as you did. But you still carry around these ghost parents inside you, and the messages, ideas about yourself, feelings, hurts, wounds, and blessings they bestowed upon you are still either haunting you or helping you in the present. Saying good-bye to your ghost parents is difficult at best, but if you don't, you will confuse those ghosts with your real, present-day parents. When you can't tell the difference, you probably regress.

Last week Earl attended one of my two-day mini-intensives. A small wiry man, Earl is a veterinarian from Washington State. His emotional range is very narrow, as he'll be the first to admit. That's why he came to see me. We worked one-on-one for several hours each day. He told me that his marriage was on the rocks. One reason for this was that after twenty years of marriage to the same "wonderful woman," he wasn't sure if he still loved her anymore. More important, she didn't feel loved by him any longer. Even though he often told her that he loved her, she had been saying for a number of years that she didn't believe him.

After several hours of consultation, we discovered that Earl's father's emotional life had also been pretty barren, in fact all but nonexistent. As we talked, he realized that his emotional desert was one of the few things he and his father had in common. His father never spent time with Earl as a boy and left his son not knowing if he really loved him. More important, his father didn't teach him the art of love. Earl explained that it was his mother who raised him and taught him what little he knew about feelings. Most boys need to learn how to love from a man, I pointed out to him, simply because men and women are, in some ways, fundamentally different.

What Earl's father taught him was how to work, and work he

did—sixty or seventy hours a week running three veterinary clinics and making more money than he could ever spend in his lifetime. "When was the last time you took your wife on a romantic vacation?" I asked.

Earl looked sad. "We haven't been on a trip that wasn't tied to my work in some way in over seventeen years," he said. "My wife's parents were also workaholics, and they taught her to be one as well. Between the two of us, we work all the time."

I asked Earl if he thought his father was proud of him for being such a success. He immediately said, "Yes."

"Earl, let me ask you something. Is working as hard as your father did a way to connect with him, perhaps to show him that you really are a 'chip off the old block'? Do you think that if he got to know you and see that you have adopted his work ethic, maybe he'd be the father you never had?"

Earl teared up.

I continued, "It may be time to say good-bye to him and to the way he taught you to put work before love. I want you to close your eyes and hold out your hands. The hands you are going to take are your father's hands." I moved closer to this fifty-year-old boy who needed to let his father go and placed my hands in his.

Earl got red in the face.

"Earl, watch what feelings, thoughts, or memories come up when I ask you to say these words: 'Good-bye, Dad. I have to let you go.'"

Earl wept deeply.

"What do you need to tell him before you let him go, Earl?"

Earl was silent for several minutes. "I need to tell you, Dad, that you should have spent more time with me and taught me how to love and to feel love. Now I've got to let you go and learn how to give and receive love before it's too late. It might be too late for you, but it's not too late for me." Earl cried some more and then let go of my (his ghost father's) hands.

One of the biggest impediments to consciously saying good-bye to a father or mother is not being able to let go of our way of thinking about them. Before Earl could let go, even just a little, he first had to tell me, "I had a perfect father who did the best he could."

Now the second part of this statement is true. His father did do the *best he could.* All our fathers and mothers did the best they could, given what they were taught and what they weren't. As I told Earl, for a few minutes, a few hours, or maybe even a few years, we have to forget what we think we know about our parents so that we can finally get at what we really feel. If we can get to what we really feel about our abandoning or smothering mothers and fathers, then we can begin the healing process, which leads to less and less regression. If we can feel how our parents did not give us the love, affection, or attention that we needed—or gave us too much of the wrong kind—then we can begin to let go of their ghost images. If we can *feel* what we really needed to feel as boys or girls but probably couldn't find the words for back then, we won't need to search for someone who will wound us in the same way our parents did.

Another great difficulty in saying good-bye to Mom and Dad comes out in every workshop I have ever presented: "But I never really *had* them to begin with. So how do I say good-bye?" When many men and women look back, they see a lonely boy or girl who never made a real connection with their parents, or perhaps with only one of them. This bond may have been minimal for a number of reasons: too many children, too much work, not enough money to go around, not enough attention to go around, or just nobody around period, especially emotionally.

When I was a kid, my dad was home a lot, but he was not really emotionally available. So in many ways, when it came time for me to say good-bye to him as a parent, it was more like saying good-bye to smoke or fog. It is hard to let go of smoke or fog. But I knew I had to let him go as best I could. To do so, I had to consciously go back to the times and places in my childhood when I wish he had been there for me, and to feel the feelings that were buried under the thick coat of armor I developed when he wasn't. When I did so, I got angry, cried, yelled, and screamed and told him all the things that I wished I could have told him.

I began the process of consciously saying good-bye to my father when I was thirty-three, after the then love of my life had just left. Laurel said, as Earl's wife had, that she just didn't feel that I really loved her. At that moment, I felt like the dad I barely knew. I couldn't feel anything at all. Just as Earl's dad had taught him to work, my dad had taught me to turn into smoke and fog.

Several weeks after we had said nearly all our good-byes, I saw Laurel and asked her to have one last cup of coffee with me. I wanted to ask her something very important. She very reluctantly agreed but kept saying that she didn't see what else could possibly be said between us. We got to our favorite café. The lights were low, and the candle burning on the table illuminated her beautiful, sad face.

"Okay. I'm listening. What is it you have to say to me that you haven't already said?"

The waiter appeared with our coffee. I wish he'd brought me my ability to feel, but that wasn't on the menu. Even if it had been, I wouldn't have known enough back then to order it. I looked into Laurel's eyes and reached deep into my brain for just the right words: "Laurel, I think we should get married."

She looked at me with utter frustration. "Why?"

"Because of all we've been through. We belong together."

That was the best answer I could come up with, and the worst answer she had ever heard. She wanted me to speak from my heart, soul, and body. Instead, I spoke from my head in a lame, last-ditch effort to get her back. Like my father, I was so afraid of feelings, emotions, and the truth that I was completely numb from the neck down. This numbness and inability to speak from my heart and body were all signs that I was regressing back to a time when feelings were seldom felt and unlikely to be heard.

I had to say good-bye to my father and learn how to reawaken my emotional body, to thaw out my frozen feelings. I had to let him go.

Still another reason it's hard to let go of a mother or father can be seen in the case of Cheryl, a friend of mine. Cheryl had a difficult time letting go of her mother, Vivienne, with whom she had lived all her life. Her mother is in her seventies, and Cheryl is in her forties. Vivienne has suffered from chronic migraine headaches all her life. Cheryl became her mother's main comforter and nurse at a very early age.

"I don't know what she would have done without me all these years," Cheryl once told me during a workshop. This was probably what her mother had told her several hundred times over the course of her life.

I asked Cheryl what she wanted most at this point in her life. She didn't hesitate one moment: "I want a good man and a family of my own."

I asked for a female volunteer to come up and help with a little exercise. Betsy came up and sat directly across from Cheryl. I said, "Cheryl, I want you to close your eyes and hold out your hands. The hands Betsy is going to give you are your mother's hands."

Cheryl closed her eyes and immediately began crying. "Oh Momma, I'm so tired of taking care of you. I'm so tired of you being sick all the time. I'm just a little girl who needs to be taken care of too. Mom, I've got to let you go, but I'm afraid you won't be all right if I do. But I need to have a relationship, and I want a family of my own before it's too late."

Cheryl repeated these and other feelings over and over, still holding on to Betsy's hands. Finally, I asked some men to come up and stand behind Betsy/Mom. I asked Cheryl to open her eyes and see the men. Then I asked the men to hold out their hands to Cheryl.

"Now, Cheryl, without letting go of your mother's hands, I want you to take the hands of one of these men."

She sobbed and sobbed. "I can't take their hands and hold on to my mother's at the same time, but that's what I've been trying to do for years. Every man that I get close to has told me that I didn't have room for him in my life. One man asked me to marry him a few years ago, and I couldn't because I was afraid to leave my mother."

"Cheryl," I said, "try saying to your mom, 'Mom I love you, and I have to let you go.'"

Cheryl cried some more and finally said, "Good-bye, Mom. I have to let you go."

She dropped Betsy's hands and took the hands of all the men who came and stood in front of her. I asked her, "Which feels better—holding your mom's hands, whom you've told me really *is* capable of getting help and taking care of herself, or these men's hands?"

She laughed. "I must admit these men's hands feel awfully good to me right now."

As I said before, saying good-bye to Mom and Dad doesn't

usually mean that you will never see them again. But in some situations, in order to really let them go, it may be necessary for you to experience a brief or extended period of not being around them. In a very few cases where the relationship is truly toxic, the good-bye could be permanent.

Years ago I had to tell my mother that I needed to not speak to her or hear from her for a while, until I felt ready to reestablish contact. My mother and I had become so thoroughly and completely enmeshed during my childhood that I no longer knew where I began and she ended. So at the tender young age of thirty-three, I needed some time away to *separate* from her. This process was terribly painful for me. We had called each other every week since I had left home at seventeen. I don't think we missed a week more than once or twice during all those years.

I was very scared. After all she was, in a way, the only real parent I'd had while I was growing up. My father, like many men of his generation, was gone most of the time, either into alcohol, work, worry, television, or all of the above. So saying good-bye to him was a lot easier than to Mom. She and I were so attached to each other that when we separated temporarily, it sounded like Velcro ripping.

Six agonizing months went by before I called her again. During this time, I was in therapy trying to come to terms with who I was apart from her wishes, wants, desires, and needs. It was not easy. Nor had I completely finished the process at the time when I called her and asked if I could come for a visit.

She met me at the airport. We hugged but didn't say a word. When we got to the car, all she said was "Would you like to drive?" She handed me the keys, and we headed toward my hometown, Tuscumbia, Alabama.

About thirty minutes into the drive, she finally broke the long silence. "You know, son, I've been reading some books and articles over the last few months, and I've been doing a lot of thinking. I've discovered that there are some things that I didn't know. One of the most important things I've learned is that you have many reasons to be really angry with me."

I nearly fell out of the car. Hitting the pavement at sixty-five miles per hour would have had less of an impact on me than what she had just said.

We talked all the way home and began to develop the foundation for a more adult mother-son relationship. We began what would eventually become a pretty nice friendship. Since then, my mother and I have worked very hard to separate ourselves, in a clean and respectful way, from the things in our relationship that don't serve us. She has done so much growing and learning, and so have I. Only a few years ago, I used to get calls where she would say, "When are you coming home to see us? We're not getting any younger and won't always be around." Now it's more like "We hope you'll come visit soon. It would be nice if you could come for Christmas, but you do what's best for you and your family. We'll be fine. But we'll miss you, and you'll be in our thoughts and prayers."

I have to admit that the more I hear the second kind of statement, the more I look forward to visiting my parents' home. The word *home* might actually serve as a litmus test for how much saying good-bye you still need to do. Do you still consider your parents' house to be *home,* or have you made a home for yourself?

Remember, letting go of your parents is not a single event but a process. When you can let your parents go and feel all the feelings that that brings up, you won't regress when someone says or does something that reminds you of Mom or Dad. More often than not, you will be able to clearly see and hear the people with whom you are present. Also, you will learn to see your biological parents as people—humans who have hurt you, helped you, or wounded you. You may even find that, in some strange way, they have helped you to become the fine person you are today if for no other reason than that they supplied you with a reverse role model.

## TO KEEP FROM REGRESSING AT FAMILY FUNCTIONS

The short answer is, don't go. Just kidding. The best way to stay an adult when visiting relatives is to remember that they are all probably regressing to some degree or another. Uncle Tim's regression may take the form of overly loud laughter. Aunt Margaret's may take the form of extreme silence in a crowd. Brother Bob's may take the form of drinking too much.

But we cannot know for sure whether others are regressing. We can only know if we ourselves are feeling small, wanting to disappear, or wanting to take over and control everything.

Something about family get-togethers brings out *the kid* in all of us. It can be fun if no one gets hurt. But acting childish usually has some negative if not disastrous consequences. There is a big difference between being *childish* and *childlike*. When adults are childlike, spontaneous, and playful, no one gets hurt. But making fun of your father is regressive and childish. Putting down a sibling is regressive and childish. Telling an old family story about Dad that does not belittle or demean him in any way can be touching, tender, and funny.

The real difficulty lies in your habits. If you put down a parent or made fun of a sibling and got a big laugh at last year's New Year's Eve party, you'll probably try it again, especially if you have not had enough attention lately or if someone has recently made fun of you.

Family patterns and roles get established very early in life. The recovery movement of the late 1970s and 1980s helped to identify distinct behaviors that are either assumed by or assigned to people in the family. In my own family, my father was the Designated Problem, my mother was the Martyr, the long-suffering "good" one. My younger sister was the Peacemaker who tried to explain and reconcile all points of view so that everyone could understand each other and therefore get along better. My younger brother was the Invisible Child who was seldom seen and very seldom heard. And me—I was the Hero who wore a cape and wanted to save the day until Mighty Mouse or Superman could find his way to our house. Even now I must double-check from time to time to make sure I'm not wearing tights and an S on my chest.

One of the best ways to stave off regression is to avoid falling back into whatever pattern or role you assumed or were assigned within the family. That is not easy. In fact, it goes against the grain. For me, being a Hero comes easy, but it is also exhausting and ultimately alienating to those who feel less than heroic.

I learned this lesson the hard way over a decade ago, when my father was still drinking. To "help" my dad, I decided to call all the members of my family together and do what is called an intervention. We would convene as a family and truthfully tell my father how we felt about his drinking and about the damage that he was doing to us as a family and as individuals. My family members agreed. Having already worked in the field of recovery for several years, I knew it would be a good idea to have a health care professional on hand to facilitate the very tricky business of confronting a loved one about alcoholic, abusive, or dangerous behavior.

I called several people I knew who were supposed to be good at leading interventions and finally decided on Mr. Brown, who had been in recovery from alcoholism for two decades and had a pretty good track record for helping families to get into recovery and support programs, even if he could not get the actual alcoholic or drug addict into treatment.

We met with Mr. Brown for a few hours the day before the intervention. To make a long story short, he identified the roles we each had learned to play in our little family drama all too well. He went around the room telling my mother, sister, and brother what to do and what not do, what to say and what not to say. I immediately became anxious because he was asking them to do things that I had never seen them do and didn't think they were capable of doing. Finally I said, "So what about me? What do I do?"

He looked at me and nailed me good. "I want you to do only two things. First, keep quiet. Don't say a word during the whole intervention. My guess is you've said enough for everyone. The second thing is, stay in your seat no matter what happens. Don't leave."

I wasn't sure if Mr. Brown had read my two autobiographical books or not, but he sure knew "a back walking away" when he saw one.

When my father arrived, everyone tried to do as Mr. Brown had instructed. The hardest thing I've ever done in my life was to go against the grain and not play the role of the Hero. I perspired, wiggled in my uncomfortable seat, and thought I would come out of my skin. My sister, brother, and mother did an excellent job of "not doing what they had always done." They were very adult and powerful. Not powerful enough to get my father into treatment, unfortunately. But my mother went into recovery, and my sister got some help as well. As for me, I learned that going against a life-long pattern is difficult but can be energizing and liberating. Now I seldom play that tiresome Hero role with my family, and we all seem to get along better.

## FOUR TIPS TO MINIMIZE REGRESSION
## AT FAMILY FUNCTIONS

### TIP 1

Know your personal rhythms and tolerances for closeness and connection, and for separation and solitude. To illustrate what a "personal rhythm" is, I'll tell you the story of a good friend of mine who has a wonderful and wise thirteen-year-old stepdaughter. One day he asked her, "How are you enjoying your visits with your real dad these days?"

She said her trips were going great. My friend thought this was odd because she usually feels pretty miserable at her biological father's house. He asked her what was different. She immediately replied that she was.

"How are you different?" he asked her.

"Well," she said, "I stay with my father for one hour, and then I go to my grandmother's for the rest of the weekend."

My friend was very surprised. "Doesn't your dad get mad that you leave so soon?"

"Yes," she said matter-of-factly, "but that's his business. Mine is to know what my rhythms are and to stay true to them. So far it's worked great for me. I enjoy seeing my dad, we don't fight, and I don't have to feel bad. An hour is all we can do right now. Maybe later we'll work up to two or three."

"Where did you learn this?" he asked this thirteen-year-old genius.

As it turns out, she had listened to my tape *The Rhythm of Closeness: How to Have True Intimacy Without Losing Yourself.*

She advised her stepfather to listen to it because "I've noticed when you go home to visit your parents, you stay the entire weekend and vow never to see them again."

She had him there. My friend admitted to me that he had never listened to that tape until he had this conversation with her. "Now I try to pay attention to my own rhythms, whether it's around my parents or with my wife. To tell you the truth, I find that I'm regressing less and less when I do this."

## TIP 2

Cut the invisible strings that keep you tied to your family in behaviors that are no longer useful. Examples of such behaviors are:

- NOT EXPRESSING ANGER AND GRIEF
- NOT ASKING FOR WHAT YOU REALLY WANT AND NEED FROM YOUR FAMILY
- KEEPING SECRETS FROM CERTAIN FAMILY MEMBERS
- TRIANGULATING, MANIPULATING, OR MANEUVERING FOR POWER

One type of invisible string is a trust fund or inheritance. Karen is one of the most likable people you'll ever meet, and she jumps through hoops to keep her father happy. She almost never disagrees with him in public, even when she knows he's wrong. She dutifully visits him every Sunday, no matter what. Why? Because he controls her trust fund.

Fear of losing an inheritance can make us regress in a New York minute. It's much easier to say good-bye to Mom or Dad if all you stand to inherit is their old mobile home parked on a little lot in Alabama. But if you feel that you have something substantial to lose, it's hard to keep to your rhythms, to stay true to yourself, and to speak your truths, especially at family functions.

## TIP 3

Keep this question in mind during family functions: *How old am I feeling right now?* In other words, make sure you do an age check before you open your mouth. Otherwise you might say something you'll regret, either for the duration of the visit or for the rest of your life. Checking in with yourself can be a lifesaver. Before you tell your loud uncle to shut up, ask yourself this question. If your answer is any age below your current age, I'd suggest you hold your tongue.

## TIP 4

Suppose you find yourself in a regression. You can't identify your own rhythms or see the invisible strings and cut them. If you forget to do an age check and you can't grab your own tongue, then remember two words—*duct tape*. We all know the virtues of this common household item. It will fix anything temporarily until it can be fixed permanently. Everyone should take a roll of duct tape with them to family functions. Right before you blurt out that thing you always say that gets you in trouble, slap a piece of tape right onto your mouth. The only hurt will be when you pull it off, and if you pull it off fast, it won't hurt at all.

Of course, I'm just kidding. But for some people, the mental/visual aid of duct tape can be a lifesaver.

# CHAPTER 5

# REGRESSION WITH AUTHORITY FIGURES

# AND IN THE WORKPLACE

For most of us, after family functions, regression is most likely to happen at work, or when someone is in authority over us. Our bosses and/or supervisors seem to be able to push our buttons faster than anyone else, with the exception of our family members. When you work with a family member, the likelihood of regression is even greater.

The single greatest reason we regress with someone in authority is that they usually remind us of a parent or someone else from our past: a teacher, minister, priest, nun, aunt, uncle, coach, or principal. In my workshops, literally hundreds of people have told me that instead of *marrying* their father or mother, they just went to *work* for him or her.

## REGRESSION WITH AUTHORITY FIGURES

An authority figure is anyone who has some amount of power, control, and say-so over us. Such a relationship contains a mutual agreement, perhaps unspoken, that by virtue of circumstance and prior arrangement there will be a certain amount of regression. Most people do not like to be told what to do, especially if they don't really feel appreciated and respected. This condition reminds too many of us of childhood: "Take out the garbage," "Clean up your room," "You don't really know how hard your father and mother work to keep this family going." Simply put, authority figures have power. The power they exercise can sometimes be benevolent and other times malevolent. In either case, the "underlings" are always in a position of having to give up some of their power to them—for better pay, for a job promotion, or just to avoid being fired.

One way of thinking about an authority figure is as the *patron*, which in Spanish means "father." Like fathers, authority figures are supposed to know what's best for us. Because of this dynamic, their power over us is similar to the power a parent has over a child. They tell us when to come to work, when to leave, and what to do when we are on the job. There's nothing wrong with that. That's *their* job. The situation only becomes unhealthy or inappropriate when that power is misused.

## THE MISUSE OF POWER AND REGRESSION

Close your eyes, and think back to the late 1990s. Many images will come to mind, but one that will take us all a long time to forget is the one of our former president, Bill Clinton, the so-called most powerful person on the planet and leader of the free world, displaying a classic case of regression regarding power and the misuse of it. Monica Lewinsky, a young, attractive woman, became an intern at the White House. Clinton took the power he held and regressed to a spoiled, adolescent boy behaving irresponsibly. Ms. Lewinsky was an adult who became small in front of such an overwhelming figure of authority and power. She became the child who couldn't say no to her boss—who was afraid to or didn't want to.

If all this weren't enough, the president took the rest of the nation with him into a major regression. Remember, regression loves company. If I'm going back to the seventh grade, I'm taking as many of you with me as I can. The media made us look at the pictures and hear the president and Ms. Lewinsky's words over and over again, like some bully who makes a young boy look at nude pictures even though he doesn't want to. We all regressed, becoming prurient adolescents who peeked into the White House windows like voyeurs. We minded everybody's business but the nation's, and other nations laughed at our childish behavior.

Clinton did have a moment where he grew himself back up and became adult enough to apologize to his fellow citizens. The following is an excerpt from the original draft of a speech that nobody got to hear. Why no one heard this speech is a matter of pure conjecture. More than likely, the people who are paid to "spin" decided the mature, straight story would do more damage to the president's ratings than the less contrite version of what happened. This is the version that was written first—Bill Clinton's apology to the American people for his "improper relationship" with Monica Lewinsky.

> My fellow Americans . . . I have fallen short of what you should expect from a president. I have failed my own religious faith and values. I have let too many people down. I take full responsibility for my actions—for hurting my wife and daughter, for hurting Monica Lewinsky and her family, for hurting friends and staff, and for hurting the country I love. None of this should have ever happened.

I never should have had any sexual contact with Monica Lewinsky, but I did. I should have acknowledged that I was wrong months ago, but I didn't. . . . What I did was wrong—and there is no excuse for it. . . . Finally, I also want to apologize to all of you, my fellow citizens. I hope you can find it in your heart to accept that apology.

Now, here is an excerpt from the speech he did give:

Good evening. This afternoon in this room, from this chair, I testified before the Office of Independent Counsel and the grand jury. I answered their questions truthfully, including questions about my private life—questions no American citizen would ever want to answer. Still, I must take complete responsibility for all my actions, both public and private. And that is why I am speaking to you tonight.

As you know, in a deposition in January, I was asked questions about my relationship with Monica Lewinsky. While my answers were legally accurate, I did not volunteer information. Indeed, I did have a relationship with Ms. Lewinsky that was not appropriate. In fact, it was wrong. It constituted a critical lapse in judgment . . . but I told the grand jury—and I say to you now—that at no time did I ask anyone to lie, to hide or destroy evidence, or to take any unlawful action. . . . It's nobody's business but ours.

I can clearly hear a remorseful adult making the first statement. The second is the speech of a regressed man who is trying to keep his numbers up in the polls. He will do whatever it takes to put the "spin" on his very improper use of power over an employee, violating the trust and friendship of other employees and the trust of the nation.

This is an excerpt from Anita Hill's testimony regarding Judge Clarence Thomas's misuse of power and authority in the workplace:

> I thought that by saying "no" and explaining my reasons, my employer would abandon his social suggestions. However, to my regret, in the following few weeks he continued to ask me out on several occasions. He pressed me to justify my reasons for saying "no" to him. These incidents took place in his office or mine. They were in the form of private conversations, which would not have been overheard by anyone else.
>
> My working relationship became even more strained when Judge Thomas began to use work situations to discuss sex. . . . After a brief discussion of work, he would turn the conversation to a discussion of sexual matters. His conversations were vivid. . . . He said that if I ever told anyone of his behavior that it would ruin his career. That was not an apology, nor was it an explanation.

One has only to read her testimony to come to the conclusion that Ms. Hill was under a great deal of stress and fear—two leading contributors to regression. For this reason, she kept silent, much as many young girls who were molested or incested by family members or friends did for decades. Ms. Hill went on to say, "Perhaps I should have taken angry or even militant steps." But she didn't. As a regressed woman, she remained quiet until she could be silent no longer.

Judge Thomas was clearly regressed when he used his power

to sexually harass Ms. Hill. Regardless of the "he said, she said" quality to this whole incident, I present it, and the Clinton-Lewinsky matter, as dramatic examples of the abuse of power and regression. These three excerpts were taken from the book *In Our Own Words: Extraordinary Speeches of the American Century*, edited by Senator Robert Torricelli and Andrew Carroll.

Another case of regression is that of Kathryn, the woman who had her employees lie to her mother if she called while Kathryn was out of the office on something other than business reasons. I can't say whether her employees minded lying for her or not. What I can say is that this is a clear case of regression, of how power can leave people feeling powerless.

## WHY THEY PUSH OUR BUTTONS

People in power and authority cause emotional regression in us not because they *have* power but because somehow we have been conditioned to believe that they have power *over us*. This conditioning is usually the result of some kind of trauma or painful incident that happened to us early in life. Somewhere in our history, we might have experienced powerlessness in the face of people, processes, or institutions. Authority figures push our buttons today because we feel this powerlessness when we are in their presence.

Jim is one of the most spiritual people I know, but until the last couple of years, he could not or would not step inside a church of any kind. Jim had been brought up to be a Christian and was a regular attendee until he was thirteen years old. During a four-day workshop, I worked with Jim on a number of issues, but not until the last day did he decide he wanted to work on some old anger that he'd been carrying around. He sat down beside me and began to talk about the day he walked out of church.

"When I was thirteen, I really loved the church. I even thought I was going to be a minister. This is really hard to talk about, but I know I have to do something about this." I encouraged him to continue. "Well, one day this little boy began to cry. The crying kept getting worse. You could see his mother was getting embarrassed, and she tried everything to get her son to stop crying. I remember looking at our minister, who was visibly upset.

"Finally, the lady took her kid out to the vestibule, and you could hear the smacks she gave him all over the church. The boy screamed even louder, and then finally there was a silence." Jim cried at this point, but he was also very red in the face. I could see he was getting angry. "Then that preacher, that so-called man of God, said, 'Now there's a mother who's not going to spoil her child and let him get away with misbehaving.' I couldn't believe he'd said that! I mean, the kid wasn't even a year old. It wasn't his fault he was crying. Anyway, I got up and walked out of that church and I never went back."

Jim was clearly very angry and needed to release some of the stored anger and tension in his body. I pulled out some pillows and placed them on a chair near Jim. Then I set another chair across from him and asked Jim to pretend that the preacher was sitting in the chair opposite.

"Jim, I want you to hit these pillows really hard and tell the preacher what you would like to have said that day instead of walking out," I said.

He looked at the pillows and then at the empty chair, filling it with the memory of that preacher from thirty years ago. He started hitting the pillows and yelling, "How dare you? How dare you? You're supposed to be a man of God. What about Jesus' words 'suffer the little children'? How could you praise that poor, ignorant mother for hitting her kid? He was just a kid."

He beat the pillows and yelled and screamed and cried for twenty or thirty minutes. Finally, he drew a deep breath and let out a long sigh of relief. "Man, where did that come from? I didn't even know all of that was in there."

"How do you feel right now?" I asked.

"I feel lighter than I have in years and not as tense. I know the guy was doing the best he could, but I didn't know just how angry I really was until today. I think I've got some more in me, but that was a good start."

About a year later, Jim called me and said that a remarkable thing had happened. A girlfriend had been trying to get him to go to church with her for a year. Finally, he went.

"And you know what, John? I actually enjoyed it. I mean, I didn't like everything about it, but it didn't bother me. And the funny thing is I might even go again. But what I don't understand is why I could go so easily when I haven't been to church in over thirty years."

"Jim, it's really simple. The church doesn't have any power over you anymore."

As soon as I said this, Jim began sobbing over the phone. He must have cried for ten or fifteen minutes. Then there was silence.

"You're right. It's so simple. Everything about the church has pushed my buttons for years—the asking for money, the hypocrisy, everything. But now it's like I can take it or leave it, but I don't have to run away from it or avoid it."

In other words, rather than being at the mercy of an old

wound, Jim finally had a choice of whether to go—or not go—to church. For many years, he had unconsciously felt that the church had power over him. When he had consciously regressed back to the time when he was hurt and angered and expressed those feelings in front of a group of supportive people, he had reempowered himself and got back his power of choice. He was able to take what was good about the church and leave the rest. That's what adults do.

I can empathize with Jim because I have similar feelings about doctors and hospitals. When I was twelve, I had pneumonia and nearly died. While I was recovering from this illness, my doctor suggested that I have my tonsils taken out. In retrospect, it was a ridiculous suggestion, but because he was the medical authority and knew what was best, my parents agreed. The doctor performed the surgery incompetently, and I came very close to death. Later, due to some other mistake in judgment, he actually had his license revoked and was sued for malpractice. Now, when I have to go to a doctor or into a hospital—which, thank God, rarely happens—I almost always regress back to being the little boy who is powerless. In the back of my mind is a small but real fear that hospitals are places for dying and not for getting well.

Just the other day I had an experience with regression and doctors. A spot on my wrist that looked like a bruise had been there for months. I finally went to see my doctor about it, and he suggested that I see a skin specialist. Reluctantly, I made the appointment. I went to the dermatologist and sat in his comfortable office feeling very uncomfortable and nervous. The fifteen-minute wait seemed like two hours. Finally, the nurse took me back to the examination room. The doctor walked in and introduced himself. He looked me over and within five minutes said that I probably had a basal cell melanoma and that it was most likely malignant and would have to be removed. Then he talked not *with* me but *at* me for another five minutes. Before you knew it, I was out of his office and in a complete state of shock. I hadn't heard anything he said except for the words "most likely malignant."

When I got home, I realized I was regressed and in a state of shock. Fortunately I knew enough to call a couple of friends and grow myself up by expressing my feelings of fear and anger at having been dismissed so quickly after being told I might have skin cancer. This emotional support enabled me to get out of my regression.

I then called the doctor and said, "I was in your office earlier this morning, and you told me that I had a cancer on my wrist. Now I want you to go over everything again, real slow this time, and I want you to answer any and all questions that I might have."

He did, and I was satisfied with his answers. They removed the cancer, and everything turned out fine. But this experience made me realize just one more time how scary doctors and hospitals can be to a boy, but how an adult can ask questions, demand more time, and keep doing so until he feels satisfied.

What authority figures still push your buttons? Where and in what circumstances? Consciously list them so that you can begin to get a handle on them. No matter how trivial or small something may sound, your pain is as big for you as mine is for me. Something much smaller than nearly dying in a hospital may push your buttons, but in reality, you can't quantify your pain, traumas, hurts, disappointments, or wounds.

## REGRESSION IN THE WORKPLACE

### How to Confront Your Boss and Not Get Fired

Your boss may remind you of an authority figure from earlier in your life, but as you work with your boss, it's important to remember that he was not present when other people or institutions hurt or disappointed you. No matter how much he may remind you of your uncaring uncle, father, coach, or drill sergeant, he is a separate person. That was the past, and this is the present. Most people who confront their boss about something do so while they are still in a regression, still angry or overreacting to the situation at hand. They forget to ask themselves, "How old am I feeling right now?" They fail to speak to their boss as an adult but end up saying things that should be said somewhere else first. And whether they realize it or not, it is not really their boss they are speaking to, but someone from their past who really pushed their buttons.

Bob works for a law firm in Dallas. As a lawyer, he's as good as they come. One day one of the senior partners, Lucas, who was also Bob's boss, came into the office in a foul mood. Lucas had just lost a huge judgment against his client and was in full regressive mode, ready to take out his defeat on anybody he came in contact with. First he scolded his secretary for bringing him lukewarm coffee. Then Bob got his wrath.

Lucas told his secretary to e-mail Bob that he wanted to see him right away. When Bob received his e-mail, all the worst-case scenarios immediately started running through his head. He was nervous, but as he told me at the workshop, "I knew I hadn't done anything to piss him off, so I went in thinking it probably wasn't that bad. Still, deep in my body I kept thinking the worse possible things." Lucas could be verbally abusive, and in truth he reminded Bob a lot of his father. So Bob was defensive as he entered the office. Lucas began by saying, "Bob we're going to have to get meaner and leaner in this office. The case you handled a couple of weeks ago should have gone better than it did. You got our client off, but your closing argument was a little weak, according to the transcripts that I reviewed."

As he listened, Bob didn't really hear what Lucas was saying, but rather all the criticisms his father threw at him during his adolescence. He became furious and told his boss that he could take his damned corporate mentality and go to hell. Bob said he was tired of always hearing what he had done wrong. He summarily got fired. Bob had finally got to say what he had always wanted to tell his father—but it cost him his job.

As he was telling me this story, I could see he was very upset and didn't have a clue as to how he could have handled it better. The first thing I asked him was "Who in your past used to always criticize you and never think you were good enough?"

Without a moment's hesitations, Bob said, "My father. I could never please that son of a bitch. He always wanted more. If I brought home four A's and a B on my report card, he would stare at it and say, 'Boy, what is that *B* doing here?' I could never do it well enough."

Bob had so much pent-up anger and resentment at his "Four A's, One B Dad" that when his boss opened a little window, decades of Bob's old anger rushed out. I had Bob consciously regress and go back and confront his ghost father, telling him all that he would have liked to say but couldn't. I handed him an ordinary bath towel and instructed him to twist it with all the anger he had been holding inside him.

Bob did as I suggested, and it was powerful. Finally, after he came back to the present, he said, "I guess I should have taken something like that towel you handed me, walked into the men's room, and twisted it to release my anger before I told my boss to go to hell."

"Yeah, Bob," I answered. "That would have been a good idea. Next time you'll know to release your anger before you get released from your job."

If your body is highly charged by something that is being said or done, remember to discharge that tension before you talk with anyone. Otherwise, you will try to use your discussion to release that tension. Before you realize it, you will probably have said much more than the situation called for. Now I'm not suggesting that you unquestioningly accept all verbal abuse. Just remember that much that triggers us is more about our history than about our present.

There are other ways to let off the steam before blowing away your boss. Write (in longhand, not e-mail) an angry letter saying all that you would like to say. Then tear it up, and throw it away. Write another one, and do the same. Take a time out—a walk around the lake. Call a trusting friend, if you are sure you will not be overheard, and tell them what an S.O.B. your boss can be sometimes. Go out to your car, roll up all the windows, and scream and yell to the point that you don't lose either your voice or your job.

## How to Confront Your Employees Without Breaking Their Spirits

Many well-intentioned, highly intelligent managers, supervisors, and bosses abuse their employees. This is usually because they themselves were abused as children, as adolescents, or as somebody else's employee. They tend to shame, blame, demean, demoralize, criticize, preach, teach, or analyze their staff instead of expressing anger, frustration, or dissatisfaction in an appropriate manner.

## CONFRONTATION

Whether we are captains of industry or the ones who clean up after everyone else has gone home, most of us are either afraid of confrontation or enjoy it a little too much. It has been my experience as a teacher and a workshop leader for over twenty years that most people tend to avoid confrontation if at all possible. They will go out of their way to keep from having to stand face to face with a friend, lover, spouse, employee, or boss. There is something inherently uncomfortable and perhaps a bit frightening about confronting someone. This is due in part to the fact that so few of us have ever witnessed or experienced a confrontation that was healthy, where neither party was in a state of regression. Thus we try to avoid it.

Bosses, however, cannot afford the luxury of avoiding confrontation. As anger builds in a work situation, so does the need for a sit-down, heart-to-heart talk. If the boss has procrastinated, then usually too much is said in the confrontation, because the issues that need to be discussed openly and honestly are too highly charged. When the boss confronts her employee too harshly, he usually regresses to the state of a small child, where spirits were broken on a regular basis. If the employee feels that his spirit is being broken, then he will usually further regress and retaliate in some way—by getting even, slacking off, sabotage, quitting, stealing, or gossiping and telling everyone what a jerk the boss really is.

### How to Keep Spirits Intact

If, as an employer, you can follow just a few simple premises, you can avoid this kind of retaliation and revenge. The first step is to make the confrontation about you and not about your employee. This is easy to say, but very difficult to remember to do. Nevertheless, it works, and keeps both yourself and your employees acting like adults and not vindictive children. Here are some important guidelines.

• It is the boss or manager's job to be clear in her communication to employees as to what is expected of them. If an employee has failed, in the boss's opinion, to carry out his assigned duties or to meet the boss's expectations of him, the adult boss will first assume that the failure was caused by her inability to express herself in a way that her employee could understand. Therefore the adult boss will explain her expectations again in another way, making sure this time that the employee has fully heard and understood her. The regressed boss, however, assumes that she has been understood and that if she hasn't been, then it's the employee's fault. The regressed manager forgets that she became a manager due to her supposedly superior abilities to communicate and manage people.

• Bosses should remember that they once walked in their employees' shoes. If they can learn to practice empathy, a clear sign of adult behavior, then they will find it easier to be a little more understanding. Regressed men and women, by contrast, forget to empathize and therefore yell and berate instead of listening and bolstering people's confidence. They make far-fetched statements such as "You're never going to get this!" instead of attempting to discover how they miscommunicated.

Making the problem about you, the employer, instead of about the employee is your most important strategy for keeping your employees' spirits intact. Here are some examples of how to do this and how not to do it:

ADULT BOSS: "John, I need to talk to you about some problems I am having. I feel that I have not communicated my expectations and needs sufficiently. I am not feeling satisfied with production or efficiency, etc., and I want to know how I could be more clear and helpful to you in completing your task."

REGRESSED BOSS: "John, you're doing a lousy job. If you don't improve your efficiency and output, I'm going to have to make some serious changes around here. Now, I don't want to scare you, but you have to figure out how to turn things around pretty damned quickly or you'll find yourself out on the streets looking for another job."

As you can see, the adult boss is not breaking John's spirit. This mode of communication will get the job done. The regressed boss is being immature, blaming, and threatening. An employee who is spoken to in this manner will inevitably regress and feel that his spirit is broken. If John does not manage to grow himself back up, he will say or do something that everyone concerned will probably regret. Possibly even those who aren't directly involved will feel the effects, including John's fellow employees, spouse, and children.

## HOW THE SELF-EMPLOYED CAN DEAL WITH AUTHORITY FIGURES

If you are lucky enough to be self-employed, you may not have to deal with authority figures as often as employees do. But they are definitely out there, and you still have to deal with them in a mature, adult way, or you will pay the price.

In some ways, the potential to regress with an authority figure might be slightly higher for the self-employed person who has no one else with whom to share the blame or responsibility for a mistake. When you are self-employed, the buck stops with you. Most authority figures know this and can use it to their advantage, should they choose to do so.

I have a very good friend who, like me, makes his living as a writer and public speaker. William is great at what he does, but about ten years ago, he regressed his face off with his publisher. After his first book was turned down by more than twenty houses, William had self-published it. After a few months, his book caught on, and people everywhere were trying to find it and buy it. Word began to get around, and his book became somewhat of a self-publishing phenomenon. Soon a large publishing house came calling, and William signed on. The honeymoon period was great. The company sold tens of thousands of copies, but soon began acting in a regressive manner, making William feel as if they had "made" his success. They started acting as if they owned him and inferred that he should be loyal to them, regardless of his situation.

They spent money on elaborate and exhausting tours for him, and he sold even more books. Then they agreed to publish his second book, which also sold in the tens of thousands. In their minds, William had become their property. They began to display this sentiment more and more openly with him, suggesting how he should dress and speak and even dictating to him what he should write next.

William believed that no satisfying book on the subject of

grief had ever been written, so he told the publisher that this was to be his next subject. His publisher, a very controlling individual to say the least (and someone whom I know personally because I have also had business dealings with him), wanted a book on anger, not grief. So William went looking for another house. Due to his successful track record, he found one immediately. Then he went back to his first publisher and told him that he still wanted to do a book on grief and that he had an offer, but he wanted his old publisher to have the right of first refusal. He wanted the same advance that his potential new publisher had offered. The old publisher went ballistic. He called William everything from ingrate to traitor to names that I won't print here.

William was more than a little stunned by his boss's behavior, and he also went ballistic. He said some things that he shouldn't have and that he regrets to this day. The publisher, out of spite and immaturity, stopped promoting William's first two successful books and omitted them from the company's catalogs altogether. The two still have not spoken to each other again.

Self-employed people are just as prone to regression as anyone else. But the key is to recognize that you must behave as an adult toward those who affect, influence, or impact your business life. Like everyone else, you are subject to some authority figure somewhere, but no individual or group authority figure has power over you. As long as you remember you are an adult, then your authority figure can bring out the big guns—threats, intimidation, and termination—and you won't feel you have to submit.

Self-employed people also need a very tightly woven support system to call on to vent their fears, frustrations, and disappointments. When you work for a company or firm, you very often have a built-in sounding board of people who really know what you're going through. As a self-employed person, you must create your own sounding board. As a self-employed writer for fifteen years, I spent lots of time and energy maintaining a group of writer friends who can empathize with me when I start regressing around how many books I'm selling or how long it takes to get the next one published.

These adults are like Jim, who realized that the church no longer had power over him. True power comes from within and goes out into the world, not vice versa. Authority figures and petty tyrants do not really have power over people. This is a regressive illusion. Power percolates and emanates from within. When we forget this and act otherwise, we are regressing.

## WHAT TO SAY ON A JOB INTERVIEW

Job interviews are fertile ground for regression. The longer you have been unemployed, the greater your potential for regression. So much importance is attached to looking and sounding good at an interview that many people become impotent to convey how qualified they are. They tend to regress, underselling themselves, or they fall into the deep black hole called "negative grandiosity" where they oversell themselves so much that a boss becomes intimidated and refuses to hire someone who is so clearly after his own job.

The adult job-seeker should come across as respectful but not too afraid or oversolicitous, available but not too needy or broke, modest but not too humble, confident but not too full of themselves or controlling, interested but not intoxicated with possibility. They state their case clearly and concisely to someone who may have power—but not power over them.

BEHAVIOR DURING AN INTERVIEW

Regressed men and women do the following during an interview:

- LIE OR EMBELLISH THE TRUTH
- ACT TOO HUNGRY
- REFUSE TO ADMIT TO THEIR WEAKNESSES
- PUT OTHERS DOWN
- NEGATE THEIR OWN ACCOMPLISHMENTS
- ARE TOO SELF-EFFACING
- ACT TOO PUSHY AND DEMANDING
- FINISH THE INTERVIEWER'S SENTENCES AND SECOND-GUESS HIM OR HER
- ARE PHYSICALLY AGITATED AND IN A HURRY TO GET THE INTERVIEW OVER WITH

Adult men and women behave this way during an interview:

- ASK MORE QUESTIONS AND TRY TO GET AS MUCH INFORMATION AS POSSIBLE
- TAKE THEIR TIME WHEN ANSWERING QUESTIONS AND DON'T FEEL RUSHED OR FOOLISH
- ANSWER TRUTHFULLY
- CITE THEIR STRENGTHS AND WEAKNESSES, BUT NEITHER IN EXCESS
- KNOW THAT JUST AS THERE IS NOT JUST ONE MATE IN THE WORLD, THERE IS NOT JUST ONE JOB FOR THEM
- ASK FOR WHAT THEY NEED AND DON'T SETTLE FOR LESS THAN THEY DESERVE

In a wonderful movie called *Defending My Life,* the comic genius Albert Brooks plays a character who has died and finds himself facing a prosecuting attorney and a panel of judges. They are showing him key scenes in his life where he made good judgments and not-so-good judgments. One scene shows him and his wife sitting at a table having breakfast. Brooks's character is asking his wife to role-play and be the prospective employer who will interview him that morning for a job in advertising. Brooks's character is qualified and experienced and knows what he needs and deserves. He insists to his wife that he can't accept a penny less than $64,000 and tells her so unconditionally as she sits across from him in her boss persona.

In Heaven, they show the playback of the meeting that occurred between Brooks and his prospective employer. Brooks is sitting across from this authority figure, who says to him, "We have an opening for a new advertising accounts position, and it pays $42,000."

Without a moment's hesitation, Brooks reaches across the boss's desk and says, "I'll take it."

## How to Resign Without Burning Bridges

Adults build bridges. Regressed men and women burn them. The bridges that get burned most often are those that span from one job to the next. Adults try to minimize the damage done to a bridge that they may need to take them back to where they began or to where they will eventually end up.

When most bosses or managers fire someone or lay them off, they forget to see the big picture. This is usually because they avoid confronting the employee until it is almost too late. When the confrontation finally takes place, a great deal of regression comes along with it, and the manager usually winds up burning all the bridges between himself and his employee.

Jason told me a great story about not burning bridges. He had recently gone to work for a large accounting firm in New York. Abe, his senior and division manager, felt a great deal of pressure from the main office to cut back on staff, and Jason saw a memo to Abe concerning cutbacks. Given the old "last hired, first fired" rule, Jason knew he might soon find himself laid off.

Abe was an essentially kind and decent man, and Jason liked having him as a boss. He remembers well the day Abe fired him.

"Abe came into the office on a Monday morning and told us that he had to let somebody go. He couldn't decide which one of us because he liked everyone there, and we all were doing a good job. So he decided to put all the employees' names in a hat and have his secretary draw one. That person would be the unlucky one who had to hit the bricks."

Jason got a little red in the face as he proceeded. "We all nervously awaited our fates, and the secretary pulled a name. And wouldn't you know it—it was mine. I wasn't too angry at the time, just a little disappointed and sad, but I felt I would get good recommendations and find another job soon.

"About a year later I ran into Abe's secretary at a bar in the Village. She had been laid off a few days before and she was a little tipsy. She remembered me, and we began talking. She told me that the firm had been closed and gone bankrupt. Everyone was on the street looking for work. I told her that I had found a senior-level accounting position and needed a secretary, and I asked her if she would be interested. She started weeping. I thought I'd said something any unemployed person would like to hear, so I asked her why she was crying. Turns out that Abe had her make out several slips of paper to put in the hat, but they all had my name on them. He had known all along who he was going to let go, but he made it appear that he was really being kind, and in a way I guess he was.

"Now, here is where the story really gets a little crazy. Who should show up at my firm, just the other day, looking for work? You guessed it—dear old Abe. I have to decide whether to hire him by Monday of next week, and I don't know how I feel about it."

I helped Jason to see and feel his anger at Abe, and to express everything he felt—the betrayal, hurt, disappointment, and sadness. Then I had him pretend that Abe was sitting in front of him as he spewed out all his feelings. After about thirty minutes, Jason breathed a heavy sigh of relief and said, "You know in the big picture, I got the job I wanted and really like. I even got a raise and a good truthful secretary. And if I recommend Abe to my boss, I've got someone who is a good accountant and who will always be in my debt. I really can't gain anything by keeping him out of a job he's clearly qualified to do, and I certainly won't be losing anything."

Jason didn't burn either the bridge or the man. He saw the big picture, and that's what adults do. There's an old saying, "What goes around comes around."

Richard is another person who doesn't believe in burning bridges. He and his wife separated amicably, and five years later she became the director of an advertising firm in Atlanta. When Richard lost his job, she immediately hired him without reservations. They work together well and are—to this day—the best of friends.

Bridges get burned when we let out too many words, or too

many pent-up feelings too often or not often enough. Every word we say that should have been hurled in some other direction makes our fuses shorter. Every unexpressed feeling of anger or sadness makes our dynamite more likely to detonate. If you don't want to explode and say things you are never able to take back, or hurl TNT (trouble, negativity, and turmoil) into your boss's office, then I suggest that you consciously regress with safe, supportive, empathic people. Remember the line from that Wallace Stevens poem: "Sometimes the truth depends on a walk around the lake." That simple action, or one like it, can defuse many a bomb bridge that's about to blow.

# CHAPTER 6

# REGRESSION WITH LOVERS AND FRIENDS

## REGRESSION WITH LOVERS

Falling in love again and again is like bungee jumping without a cord tied to your feet. We almost always hit the ground hard, but the free fall into the unknown is worth it. Why do you think they call it "falling" in love? Falling in love is the greatest of all regressions. We fall back to sometime that doesn't even have a name. We fall back into the arms of a good mother; we descend into the comfort we knew in utero. We fall out of time and space. We fall out of care for the banal, menial, and ordinary things in our lives.

### FALLING IN LOVE—THE ULTIMATE REGRESSION

One reason falling in love is the ultimate regression is that we lose much of our control over our own bodies. During the first three to six months of a new relationship, your head can only nod up and down in agreement with everything your newly beloved says or does.

"You like coffee?" your beloved asks.

Your head bobs up and down like the little plastic dog on the dashboard of your father's old Chevrolet.

"You like to go to the movies?"

Your head uncontrollably nods in agreement.

"You breathe air?"

"Wow, now that's incredible—so do I!"

During the first few months of this wonderful regression, a woman can even get a man from Alabama to say that he too loves the ballet.

On a more serious note, when you first fall in love, your mouth may become dry, your heart beats faster, your skin flushes a brilliant red. Even your pupils dilate as if you were on drugs— because indeed you are. The seratonin levels in your brain are flowing like a raging river, your pheromones are dancing in dizzying circles, and your testosterone or estrogen levels go up. Adrenaline has to pump through you nonstop just to keep up with the demands the new romance places on your body. You very likely can't sleep, you're not very hungry, and you feel better than ever. Many people become romance addicts because all the biochemical and neurological changes feel so pleasant. Most adults like the feelings that come with the regressive act of falling in love, which is why they return to drink from Aphrodite's sweet well time and time again. After that water touches their lips, they are free to be like children—spontaneous and sensual, able to savor each minute with the beloved. Who in their right mind would refuse this and not shout, "Felix culpa!" (Latin for "fortu- nate fall"), especially since we all know it's not going to last for- ever. The fall and the feelings that accompany it always come to an end. But why?

One reason is that we fall in love only with the familiar, which, as I mentioned earlier, hearkens back to the family. Falling in love is really another way of returning to the biological family nest. Many will object to this idea and say their new love doesn't remind them at all of their parents or ex-lovers. But a year later most of these will admit that they have married, or become committed to, their mother or father yet one more time. Falling in love is a regressive act, and regression means you feel that you don't have a choice. The adult equivalent is to *choose love.* If you are going to love, live with, or marry someone who will be the culmination of both the good and the bad that you were raised with, you might just as well learn to choose.

As children, we couldn't pick our parents. I always loved the New Age idea that we pick our parents before we are born. But I don't believe it, because I like to think of myself as reasonably intelligent. If I were able to pick a dysfunctional family, I would have picked the Fords, Gettys, or Rockefellers. At least I would have been better able to pay for therapy.

Many people I've worked with over the years give themselves away when they say "I married him [or stayed with him] because I didn't have a choice." Adults always have a choice. Adults, unlike children, have car keys and access to credit cards, checking accounts, or cash. They can always leave a relationship or a marriage if it's not working out. Adults can get help—therapy, treatment, and support groups. If they feel they can't choose, they are regressed.

The other night at a lecture a man raised his hand and said, "Is it possible that you can be in a regression your whole life and not know it?" Everyone in the room, including me, laughed. We all knew that in some areas of our life, we have been in a deep regression, perhaps for decades. The sad truth is that when it comes to the whole falling-in-love thing, most of us only have a few TMMs (temporary moments of maturity). And the best TMM you can have is to finally give up the ghost of the perfect partner, say good-bye to the notion of "love at first sight," and make a conscious decision to choose love.

## Choosing to Love

In the Far East, there is a saying: "Westerners marry the person they fall in love with. In the East we love the people we marry." While so many songs, poems, and popular films tell us there is no greater insanity than falling in love, older cultures (especially indigenous cultures and tribes) suggest a different approach to loving. You may be surprised to learn that nearly two-thirds of the earth's population still engages in arranged marriages. These predestined romances are often set up before birth by the elders of a people. Now I'm not saying they are right and we are wrong. But think about all the people you *thought* were right for you and how they turned out—well, let's just say, less than right.

When we get into this topic in my workshops, I ask the participants a question: "How many of you knew in the first three to six months that the person you were going to marry was really not right for you but you married them anyway?" Many hands shoot up, even though some are embarrassed to raise them. Then I ask, "How long did you stay with them before it ended in a breakup or divorce?" You'd be surprised at the number of people who answer fifteen, twenty, or twenty-five years. To add a touch of lightness to this heavy moment, I always give a free copy of one of my books to the person who hung in there the longest. They laugh—but I'm sure that "hanging in there" caused them a lot of pain and grief. No wonder it's called "hanging."

Did they choose love if they stayed for twenty-five years? I'd like to say yes. But in most cases, the real reasons people stay together are:

- FOR THE KIDS
- FEAR OF BEING ALONE
- FEAR OF CHANGE
- FEAR OF FINANCIAL RUIN
- BECAUSE THEY TOOK VOWS
- HOPE THAT THINGS WOULD CHANGE OR THAT THEIR PARTNER WOULD CHANGE

Many people who follow the twelve-steps traditions of AA and Al-Anon have a saying: "Insanity is doing the same thing over and over again and expecting different results." I can't tell you how many people stay in a relationship because they thought if they worked, tried, or prayed a little harder, it would get better.

Choosing love is what adults finally learn to do after they have wrecked their bodies, souls, and psyches and perhaps wreaked havoc on too many other bodies, souls, and psyches. Choosing love sounds less romantic than falling in love, and it's a lot less crazy—"Crazy, crazy for feeling so lonely, crazy for feeling so blue," sings Willie Nelson. The problem is that when you're crazy in love, you don't know just how regressed you really are. You're slacking off on your job, burning the candle at both ends, and usually spending far more money than you can afford, and your mind is writing checks your body can't cash. Choosing, on the other hand, requires consciousness and support. Adults who choose love clearly communicate to their beloved what they need, want, tolerate, and dislike. Choosing love requires setting boundaries and keeping yourself intact while loving another. In the long run, it is much better than the temporary feeling of falling in love. Indeed, *conscious* loving actually deepens as time goes on.

Think about this: What if you could make love to your best friend? What would that be like? Many of you reading this do not know. You are making love with your husband, lover, or wife without having really gotten to know him or her. But lovers who choose love—instead of letting Cupid, Venus, or the penis do it for them—make love to someone who is also their best friend.

In a recent study on attraction, Dr. Patricia Love found that if you are physically and sexually attracted to ten people and you do not act on that attraction but rather take time to get to know all of them, at the end of three to six months you will still be attracted to only three out of those ten. When we teach our Post-Romantic Stress Syndrome workshop two or three times a year, she explains the biochemical component of this equation, and I add the personality component. After three to six months of really getting to know someone, we find out their character flaws, personality quirks, dysfunctional behaviors, and other things that simply turn us off. But if we are led by romance novels or our genitals, we are not able to see these things clearly. As we all know, love is blind. At least new love is.

Choosing love means making an adult decision to be "friends first." Most couples let the heat of passion and quick attraction take them down lovers' lane, which is a dead end. But Friendship Drive is a circle. When friendship is the driving force, we discover the many facets of our loved one's personality. We go through time with this lover/friend and find that, if we are both growing and changing, we have both become many different and exciting people along the way. To choose love is to say, "I want to know you. I want to like you. I want to know if we can be friends before I sleep with you and make love to you."

Many of you will say this is old-fashioned. Maybe it is. But the truth is, with the divorce rate at one couple out of two, and so many marriages ending up like schoolyard brawls, you might want to give this a try.

One of the main reasons that adults choose love is so they will not have to say or listen to these words after a marriage or a live-in relationship ends—"Now let's try to be friends." The one who instigates the leaving, by the way, usually speaks these words. Choosing love puts friendship at the beginning rather than the end. Hopefully, if the relationship has developed into a close friendship, the friendship will still be there at the end instead of bitterness, resentment, or hostility. But remember, most adult behaviors, like choosing love, require time. Falling in love can be done in a moment, a minute, or a month, but choosing love takes time. You get out of something what you put into it. If you put in months to build a solid friendship, chances are you're going to get a lot out of it.

## SENDING YOUR PARTNER THE KIND OF LOVE HE OR SHE WANTS

I thought I knew what my first wife wanted when it came time to show her that she was loved. I found out too late that I was wrong. You see, most regressed men and women send what they themselves would have liked to receive as a child, and because they very often didn't get what they wanted or needed, they are still seeking it by sending it. For example, suppose my parents withheld sweets from me as a child (even with my best interests at heart, so as not to give me cavities), but I really have a sweet tooth that goes unsatisfied. When I grow up, I'll send my sweetheart (who doesn't have a sweet tooth) a box of chocolates.

Then when she doesn't eat them—I will. Does that sound too simple? Okay, let's take it up a notch or two. You really need to talk, so you ask your mate if she wants to talk about a problem. She says no. But you keep asking over and over again until she has to scream at the top of her lungs, "NO! I don't want to talk. I have nothing I want to say!" Still too simple? Okay, how about when you are always offering to give your girlfriend a massage and she keeps refusing, but you keep asking and she keeps refusing. Isn't it possible that you are the one who needs to go to a massage therapist every week and get the very thing that you are so desperately trying to give?

This regressive way of trying to get what we want by giving it is taught to us as children. It is even implicit in the Golden Rule—"Do onto others as you would have others do onto you." Some have said there is a higher Platinum Rule—"Give onto others what they want, and ask them to give onto you what you want." This new rule is the adult way to approach love. It creates long-lasting, best-friend relationships.

Think about your best friend for a moment. What kind of love do you send to her? The answer is probably the kind she needs and wants. Now think about the ways in which your friend shows you how much she loves you. The truth is, she sends you exactly what you need. Friends do this for friends. But romantic lovers usually regress and send what they themselves would like to receive. That's why at the end of a relationship, they say, "Now let's try to be friends." In other words, let's give each other what we really need whenever possible. When friends stop sending each other what they need and want, they usually stop being friends. Everyone reading this has experienced the loss of a good friend. They changed, you changed, their needs changed, or yours did, and so they moved on to find someone new who could engage in the mutual dance.

## Asking Your Partner for the Kind of Love You Need

A few years ago, I was presenting my material on regression at a five-day intensive in New York. A lovely couple who had been married for twenty-eight years attended. They were extremely vibrant and curious, and both were in their seventies. On the fourth day, I asked them if they would be willing to participate in a little exercise. They both agreed.

"Irene," I started, "what would you like from your husband right now at this very moment? Just close your eyes, and see what comes up."

She closed her eyes, and Gary rolled his. His expression had "What have I gotten myself into?" written all over it. Irene took a deep breath and said to her husband, "I'd like for you to touch me."

Without a moment's hesitation, Gary reached over to her and put his hand on her knee. They sat there for about five minutes in silence. The rest of the group got a little irritated because they couldn't see why I was waiting so long and wasn't moving on to something else. Finally I asked Irene, "Is that where you wanted to be touched?" She shook her head no. "Where did you want to be touched?"

"Well, I just love it when he takes his big old hand and gently cups the back of my neck. It feels so good."

"Why didn't you ask him to move his hand from your knee and put it on your neck?"

What would you have answered? I asked the group, who now understood why I did the exercise, how they would respond. These are the answers they gave:

- YOU'D THINK AFTER TWENTY-EIGHT YEARS OF MARRIAGE HE WOULD KNOW.
- SHE DIDN'T WANT TO EMBARRASS HIM.
- SHE WAS JUST GLAD SHE GOT TOUCHED AT ALL AND DIDN'T WANT TO PUSH IT.
- SHE WAS AFRAID HE'D WITHDRAW AND GO SILENT.
- SHE IS PROBABLY USED TO SETTLING FOR WHAT SHE GETS.

These were just some of the many answers they gave. When I asked Irene if any of them were true for her, she answered, "All of them."

Regressed men and women are afraid to ask for what they want. This is usually because, as children, they learned that they were not going to get most of what they asked for. A study done some years ago showed that by the time a child is two, he or she has heard eighty-five *nos* for every *yes*.

Self-esteem is also important in asking for what you want and need. Recently a client was telling me that he wished his wife was more attentive to his needs, and especially was more nurturing and gentle.

I asked him one question: "Do you feel deserving of more nurturing and gentleness?"

He was silent for a while. "Well, I give her a lot of nurturing and gentleness whenever I can."

"But that wasn't the question. The question is, do you feel you deserve it just because you are you? Not in exchange for something you have done?"

Asking your partner for what you need is based on the adult feelings of sufficiency, security, and self-esteem, all of which make the adult feel "worthy." Many adults do not feel worthy unless they do something to deserve it. Some of you, as children, may have felt that you didn't deserve dessert unless you ate all your vegetables or cleaned your plate. Or that you didn't deserve the right to go out and play unless you cleaned up your room first. You didn't deserve to inherit the farm unless you worked your fingers to the bone. In other words, so much of what was given to you was given with strings. It was a tit-for-tat system of giving and receiving.

A very important component of meeting each other's needs is healing yourself enough to recognize that others have needs and that you have finally matured enough to know this and to be able to ask them what they are. Sometimes this takes years of psychotherapy and reading dozens of books on relationships. Once we know that *others* have needs, we work on improving our self-esteem until we are ready to ask right out loud for our needs to be met. We are specific and we trust that we deserve to have someone meet those needs.

I often have my workshop participants do a little exercise that you might want to try. I call it the Upgrading Exercise. Those with low self-esteem close their eyes and pretend they are going to fly to their favorite destination. I have them visualize themselves crawling into the cargo hold of an airplane. I ask them to feel how cold or hot and uncomfortable it is. After a few moments, I ask them to take the last seat on the last row in the coach section and sit there for a while listening to the engines roar on the other side of the wall. Then after a few more moments, I have them move up to the center of coach and take an exit aisle seat that gives them a little more legroom. After a few more minutes, I ask them to move themselves to the bulkhead row, the one nearest to first class. Finally I ask them to go into first class and take any seat they want and order a glass of champagne to celebrate moving from cargo to first class. Many never make it out of coach, but they are working on it.

I do this little exercise mainly to get people to see where they have been most of their lives. If you have been diminished and demeaned a good portion of your life, you may continue to demean and diminish yourself without anyone's help. Let's say you have put a lot of time and effort into improving yourself for the last few years. You still may see yourself as you were twenty years ago, rather than the way people who know you see you now.

Many people are afraid that if they are seen to have needs, they will be "too much" for others or come across as "too needy." Both of these are impossible. There is not a single person on the planet who is "too needy." Many people have many needs, but they have too few people in their lives to meet them. For example, Thomas's wife tells him all the time that he is just too needy. His wife is the only person he really trusts and confides in, and that feels like too much for her sometimes, so she regresses and shames him for having so many needs. An adult would help Thomas increase his circle of friends or create a support system so that he could spread his needs around and to do the same for others.

If you didn't receive the kind of love that you needed as a kid, chances are you will not feel deserving of it as an adult. When someone does love you the way you need to be loved, it can throw you into a regression and perhaps make you distrust the person's motives or sincerity. Many children, like myself as a boy, were taught (consciously or unconsciously) that in order to survive the chaotic family system, they had to know what other people needed. For instance, I could guess with great accuracy that my mother needed a neck massage, and I could see at a hundred feet that what my dad needed was to be left alone. By the time I was six or seven, I felt I could read my family pretty well and determine their needs from a distance and try to fulfill those needs as best as a child can do. I know this may sound like an exaggeration, but it's true. The first time a woman said to me, "What is it that you need from me?" I was thirty-three years old. I remember thinking, *No one has ever asked me this before, and I don't have a clue as to what the answer is.* I was ashamed, awakened, and awkward, and I finally said, "I'll have to get back to you on that."

I guess all of this goes a long way to explain why these lines from the thirteenth-century poet Rumi mean so much to me: "The breeze at dawn has secrets to tell you—Don't go back to sleep. You must ask for what you really want—Don't go back to sleep."

## Transforming a Romantic Relationship with Minimal Regression

Sometimes a relationship truly is not working. That may be the case for you right now. If you still feel that you want to continue some kind of relationship with this person, then it needs to take a different form. There are steps you can take to increase the probability of success.

First off, be sure *with whom* you are really in conflict. Perhaps your partner reminds you of your father (or mother or ex-lover), and you are ending the relationship because he is triggering you just as your father (or mother or ex-lover) used to do. Instead of consciously regressing and really owning the old feeling, you end the relationship with your partner. Countless numbers of people have made huge decisions to move out, end a relationship, or divorce while they were in a major Trance Regression. Their partner had been pushing so many buttons, hurling them back into their past, and unconsciously reminding them of one or more people for so long that they had stopped actually seeing that person a long time ago.

A woman named Sabrina told me that several years after divorcing her husband she had realized that she needed to divorce her father and say good-bye to that unhealthy relationship. Up until then she had just kept finding guys who could never live up to her image of her dad, so she kept divorcing them and looking for him.

Brad was Sabrina's last "less than Daddy," and he tried so hard. They both had worked with me in workshops, seen great therapists, and done couples counseling. No one could convince her that her problems stemmed from the fact that, a long time ago, her father had emotionally incested her and used her as his girlfriend.

Sabrina's father, Henry, was very unhappy and unfulfilled in his marriage. Sabrina's mother, Mary, suffered from anorexia and weighed about eighty-five pounds—at nearly five foot five. Henry was ashamed of Mary's looks and was embarrassed to be seen with her in public, so he began taking his daughter everywhere. When Sabrina became a teenager, he even jokingly introduced her as his date. He treated her like a princess, buying her everything money could buy and withholding nothing except functional fatherly love and boundaries. It took her four marriages and many grueling hours of work to realize that her father shouldn't have done this to her and that she was never going to find a man who would measure up to him. Finally, in our last workshop, she realized that it was her dad who didn't measure up to the standards of a good father, and that the men she had been with were mostly kind, gentle, nice guys who were doing the best they could given the situation. As she grieved, she said, "Actually they were good husbands, but my father wasn't a good husband to my mom and wasn't a good father to me."

A similar scenario has been brought to my attention many times by men who were their mother's confidant, surrogate husband, and counselor. Many of these regressed mothers convinced their sons, quite unconsciously, that they would never find a "girl just like the girl who married dear old dad."

## REGRESSION WITH FRIENDS

Sometimes even the best relationship can seem like a battlefield mined with regression bombs waiting to be stepped on. The truth is, there isn't any war. If your friend is touchy, weepy, or angry, it's usually not because of anything you have done personally. It's just that these bombs were planted a long time ago, probably long before your friendship began.

A couple of years ago, Allen, a colleague and good friend of mine, and I were teaching a course on modern poetry. We were invited to the Library of Congress to give a reading and were allotted thirty minutes each. Because we got started late, Allen didn't get his full thirty minutes, but I did. As we were leaving the building, I noticed something was bothering him. "What's the matter?" I asked innocently. I really didn't have a clue.

Allen looked at me. "You got all your time, and I was short-changed," he said. "My older brother used to do this to me all the time. Next time I read first."

I was taken aback. "I'm fifteen years your junior, so how in the hell can I remind you of your older brother?"

He paused. "My mother always favored him and gave him more attention than me," he said. "For a few minutes, it felt like I was back at home and you were my brother. I guess I was regressing."

Allen and I had talked a lot about regression, and he caught what he was doing. Within a few minutes, he was back to being the adult that I knew and loved, and I was no longer his brother who had received more than his fair share of attention.

## GOING SLOW WITH YOUR FRIENDS

Remember your friends from early childhood? You met them in a schoolyard, at the neighborhood playground, in an open field, by a lake, or at a birthday party. You had known each other for less than an hour when you declared yourselves to be friends for life. And some of you remain friends to this day. That's the way it was for many of us in childhood.

In adulthood, many people rush into new friendships just as they did when they were children. They meet and talk and decide they have a lot in common. Someone will say, in so many words, "Hey, let's me and you be friends. Whaddya say?" Usually the other person will say yes but may soon regret that answer. Why? Four-year-olds don't have many complications, idiosyncrasies, bad habits, personality quirks, jealous wives or husbands, and huge responsibilities. But adults do. It takes time to learn who someone really is and is not. Moving fast does not give us the time or information we need to make an adult decision to form a lasting friendship.

There is another road that many people take toward the city

of friendship. This path is particularly common among adult children from dysfunctional families or newly recovering addicts or alcoholics. On this very slippery road, you tell a potential new friend everything bad that you have ever thought, fantasized, or done, to see if they look horrified and run screaming in the opposite direction. If they don't then they usually proceed to tell you everything they have done, things that would burn most Catholic priests' ears and incinerate the confessional booth. The common term for this process of confession is "being rigorously honest." I call it being in a hurry. And being in a hurry usually points to regression.

Adults take time forming friendships, especially if they want them to last. They give a little and get a little, give a little more and get a little more. Adults see the quirks and kinks and decide if they can deal with them. If they feel safe enough, then they proceed to reveal a little more.

Sometimes people I've enjoyed meeting will say something like "Looks like we have a lot in common. Let's be friends."

And I say very respectfully, "Have you got a year or two?" The ones who look confused or disappointed are probably not going to want to go at the speed that suits me at age forty-eight, instead of the speed that suited me at four.

## BEING ACCEPTED AS YOU ARE

One major red flag of regression to watch out for in friendships is the friend who keeps trying to change you or fix you. A true friend will not treat you like her latest project of helping someone to rise to their full potential. (That project is usually saved for the one you love. "Hi, I'd like you to meet my new project— I mean, boyfriend." Just kidding.)

As you can tell by now, I love to go to the dictionary to see how words are defined. The *American Heritage Dictionary* defines *friend* as "A person whom one knows, likes and trusts . . . A person with whom one is allied in a struggle or cause; a comrade."

*A person whom one knows, likes and trusts. A comrade.* Do you see how friendship takes time and why it is necessary to go slow? I can't tell you how many people over the years have said something like this about a new acquaintance: "It feels like I have known this person my whole life." Or "I can't explain it, but we're, like, soul mates." They don't say the latter that often in Alabama, but I do hear it a lot in California.

I want to make an important distinction here between *acquaintances* and *friends*. First, let me explain that I lived in Tuscaloosa, Alabama, and taught at a university there for four years. Tuscaloosa and the university are small, and you pretty much run into everybody fairly regularly. Because I said hello, how are you doing, and got invited to parties, I thought I had literally dozens and dozens of friends. Looking back, I realize that I had lots of acquaintances. These people didn't really know me, because we didn't take the time or make the effort to really connect on an intimate level. So we really didn't trust each other, and we were not comrades. Out of all those dozens and dozens of so-called friends, only one kept in touch with me for a few years after I moved to Austin.

When I got married in a little place called Mentone, Alabama, over five years ago, I invited several of those friends from the university. I also invited my old friends who knew me and accepted me as I am. The church, I am happy and honored to say, was full of friends from my childhood, from Austin, and from around the world. But not a single person from Tuscaloosa came, even though they lived closer than anyone else to the church.

Many of us have acquaintances, but friends who really know us and really accept us as we are are scarce, few and far between. I believe I have maybe seven or eight friends who totally accept me as I am. I could tell them anything, and I know it wouldn't change their opinion of me or their love for me.

## Accepting Your Friends As They Are

Just as you don't need or want to be fixed, changed, or disparaged, neither do your friends. They want what many of us did not get as children: to be accepted as they really are—as their unique, precious self—not as what you think they should be.

When friends don't accept each other as they are, they are usually regressing, falling into patterns of judging, analyzing, teaching, or preaching. Remember, these are all signs of inappropriate anger, which can destroy a friendship faster than a speeding bullet. If a friend is angry with someone, he must stay in his adult place and confront the friend in a way that will do as little damage as possible to the friendship.

Friendships are not static and won't always be the same. Indeed, friendships should be dynamic, growing and changing like all living things. This means adults must do their best to be flexible, resilient, tolerant, and patient.

## Regression and Old Friends

It is pretty easy to regress with new friends, but not nearly as easy as it is to fall way back into our past with old friends. Dane, Roger, Bob, and I have been good friends for thirty-seven years. We've seen each other through the best of times and the worst of times. All of us have changed in many ways and have also stayed the same in many ways. When we are together, we fall back into the same behaviors we displayed when we were kids. Two hours with these guys, and we're acting as goofy and silly as ever. We probably say things that we wouldn't say anywhere else, at least not in the same way.

We tell old stories and relive precious, fleeting moments that exist only in memory. This, by the way, is one of the good things about regression—it allows you to wander the halls of memories that are not only painful but also pleasurable and fun. But if the past is the only glue holding a relationship together, and you have nothing shared or held in common in the present, the relationship will probably come apart fairly soon.

## SOME FRIENDS ARE FOREVER, SOME ARE NOT

Many friendships begin in regression and never mature out of it. A fellow I know named Ronald used to be friends with a guy named Gene. They grew up together in the same small town in Alabama. They had been friends for nineteen years when Ronald decided to quit drinking, join AA, and begin psychotherapy. Every time he would visit Gene, Gene would tease Ronald and try to get him to drink again. When Ronald wouldn't succumb to the taunts, Gene made fun of him. Finally, Ronald realized that their whole relationship was really based on beer, bars, sarcastic put-downs, and intellectual one-upmanship. Ronald talked to me and the men's group I was leading about his dilemma. We supported Ronald telling Gene that he—Ronald— needed his encouragement to continue to stay sober, and that they were going to have to build a new relationship based on something other than immature behavior.

When Ronald spoke frankly to Gene about this, Gene said,

"That's bullshit AA therapy talking. Let's go get some beer and have some fun like we used to, you pansy."

Needless to say, Ronald visited Gene only a couple of more times and finally made the decision to end the friendship. It was hard, especially because Ronald was the godfather of Gene's baby girl. In the group, Ronald wept about the loss of this friendship and the fact that he would never see his goddaughter again. I asked one of the men in the group, Rudy, to pretend to be Gene for a few minutes. Rudy agreed. Ronald went over to him and looked him in the eyes; he was consciously regressing back to a time when they used to be friends. Now he began to get angry. He turned red in the face. "Gene, how dare you not respect me and my sobriety!" he said. "Either accept me as I am, or leave me the hell alone. Screw you, you arrogant bastard." Ronald took a deep breath, and his whole body relaxed. He smiled at Rudy and then looked at me and calmly asked if he could now pretend Rudy was Gene in the present. "I need to say something else I feel, now that I'm back in the present." Ronald said, "Gene, I really miss you. You were a very important part of my adolescence, and I wish you were still in my life. I also want to say I'm sorry I don't know your daughter and that I have failed her as a godfather. I wish there were some way for us to meet and connect again. I'm going to give you a call and reach out one more time. There's nothing lost by trying, and who knows—we all change."

# CHAPTER 7

# GOOD PARENTING—RAISING CHILDREN

# WITH MINIMAL REGRESSION

There is nothing like raising a child to show you just how child-ish you can become at the drop of a diaper. Men and women are taught how to build bridges and computers, but most people are not taught how to be parents. They learn by modeling their own mom and dad. We tend to parent either in the way we were parented or its opposite. Neither usually is satisfactory to either the parent or the child. This chapter will help you minimize the amount of time you spend in regression with your children and help put an end to what Alice Miller calls "poisonous pedagogy": the antiquated belief that children are chattel and have no rights, and that the only way to control them is through strict punishment.

## THE DIFFERENCE BETWEEN BEING A PARENT AND BEING A MOM OR A DAD

If you are reading this, I can assume that you received enough food, shelter, clothing, and education to at least have survived childhood and adolescence. The minimum job of parenting is to provide sufficiently for a child's well-being so that the child is neither locked up nor removed from their home by the courts. But even though this is what most of us received, we needed and wanted much more from the people we loved the most.

*Parent* is defined in the *American Heritage Dictionary* as "one who begets, gives birth to . . . ; an organism that produces or generates offspring." Parenting is difficult and draining, but it is pretty much an automatic-pilot performance, rooted in how we ourselves were raised. The dictionary defines *mom* as someone who "watches over, nourishes and protects . . . maternal love and tenderness." It defines *dad* as a "protector." Both of these roles are harder and more time consuming than that of a parent, but they are much more rewarding and much less damaging to oneself and one's offspring. It's worth the effort to learn and practice the difference between the two. Being an adult, mature mom or dad means being able to think on your feet and knowing when to go to others for information and guidance. It means making sure that your past angers and hurts don't spill over into your child's body and soul.

Remember the man who wept over spanking his child when he caught him playing near the street? He himself was spanked as a boy. Remember the woman who cuddled with her six-year-old son because she missed her husband? Her parents used her the same way. We practice what we've been taught. We pass on what we've learned. Our children do not take after strangers.

Jane is a thin, short woman with gray hair. She is fifty, but looks fifteen years younger. According to Jane, "I had pretty good parents. I just can't figure out why I was always so hard on my kids. They were so precious, and I was such a perfectionist.

Everything had to be in order and clean—especially my kids. Now I watch them with their children, and they are doing the same thing. They're not letting them be kids. They're making them into little clean adults, and I don't know what to do. Should I say something to them or mind my own business?"

"Who taught you to be a perfectionist who always had to keep everything orderly and clean?" I asked.

Without a moment's hesitation, she said, "Why, my mother."

Jane had never fully experienced or expressed her anger and sadness at having lost a childhood to a perfect parent. So when her children did something that was less than perfect, she would express that pent-up anger toward them. In other words, she would regress back to the time she was a little girl and criticize her children. Most regressed people parent their children in the same way that they were parented.

Phil, on the other hand, parented just the opposite way from his parents. Phil is a college professor who treated his only son like his best friend instead of his child. Phil always wanted his dad to hang out with him and do things with him. But Phil's father was rarely home. He was too busy working, paying the bills, and putting a roof over his family's head, clothes on their back, and food on the table. When he was home, he was cruel and temperamental.

Phil swore he would never be that kind of parent. Instead, when he became a father, he took a 180-degree turn. He involved himself in every part of his son's life—to the point where his son ran away from home at age thirteen. Phil's son, Scott, didn't get either a parent or a dad—he got a buddy. Scott had plenty of buddies, but he wasn't getting discipline or direction at home.

Phil said, "He came back about a week before I came to this

workshop, and he's with his mother now. She and I are divorced. I know I'm angry with him for running away and not wanting to live with me anymore. So I thought I'd better do something."

"What would you like to have had from your father when you were a boy?" I asked.

"I just wanted to know him and him to know me. But it was as if he hated me. He didn't want to spend time with me. I hate him for that now. I see that I overcompensated and turned my son into my dad. I even named my kid after my dad. I tried to get from my son what I wanted from my father, instead of being the dad I should have been."

By now Phil was pounding the pillow with his fists and weeping. "I just wanted you to like me!" he yelled. "I just wanted you to know me! I just wanted you to want to be with me!" When he was finished, he looked at the group and me and said, "I don't have a clue how to be a good father."

Peter, another man in the workshop who was obviously touched, said, "Now you can start learning. It's not too late for Scott. You'll never have the father you wanted and needed, but Scott might still have a chance."

If you couldn't laugh and be spontaneous when you were a child, then when your child laughs and is spontaneous, it might throw you into a regression. If you couldn't cry because you were told things like "If you don't stop crying, I'll give you something to cry about," then when a child cries, it will make you regress. You will want that child to stop crying just as you had to, even if it is not your own child. If you weren't allowed to show your anger, then when a child shows his, that might be all it takes to regress you. You will demand that he stuff his anger into his little body just as you had to.

The following examples more clearly delineate the difference between being a regressed parent and being a mature and in-the-present mom or dad.

Six-year-old Martin rides his bike in his new blue jeans and falls off. He cuts his leg and tears his jeans.

PARENT: "I can't believe you disobeyed me about wearing your new jeans out to play. Look at those jeans! Money doesn't grow on trees, you know. Let me see your leg. Oh, it's not that bad. You'll be all right. You're not dying—now stop crying."

MOM OR DAD: "Oh sweetie, did you hurt your leg? Let me take a look at it. I'll bet that hurts. Let's see what we can do to make you feel better. Let me give you a hug, and then we'll get that leg cleaned up." [*Next day*] "How's your leg? Now next time I hope you'll be more careful and remember to only wear your old jeans when you play. If you don't, then you won't get to ride your bike for a whole day."

PARENT to a three-year-old: "Look at this mess. You've put crayon marks all over this wall. What am I going to do with you? You clean up this mess. Give me those crayons, and go to your room."

MOM OR DAD: "Wow! Look at what incredible pretty pictures you drew on the wall. You are very talented. I think I may have a little artist on my hands so I'm going to get lots of big sheets of white paper and tape it onto the walls in your room so that you can draw everything you want. I'm proud of you."

MOM OR DAD, after repainting the wall: "Now sweetie, remember to only draw on the paper that we hung on the wall for you, okay?"

How many of you had *parents* and how many of you had *moms* and *dads*?

PARENT to an eleven-year-old son: "Now if you don't stop whining about how cold it is, I won't bring you fishing with me again. I'll leave you home with your mother next time."

MOM OR DAD: "Now if you get too cold, you let me know and we'll stop and get warm so that you'll be ready to catch the biggest fish of the day."

PARENT to a six-year-old: "It's time you learned to swim today." [*Throws the child off the dock.*]

MOM AND DAD: "You let me know when you're ready to learn how to swim, and I'll go slow and teach you so you'll never be afraid of the water. Or we'll get you swimming lessons when you're ready."

All of the above are true parent stories that I have listened to over the years. I heard one of the worst ones recently in an airport as I was on my way home from New York. The parents of a four-year-old child said to him, "If you don't behave, I'll leave you here."

By now you can hear the regressive quality in these parental messages. The tone is heavy and weighted down by shame, guilt, criticism, and judgment. Contrast this with the tone of the mom or dad, which is compassionate, considerate, and careful not to damage the child's psyche or soul.

## ONLY ADULTS CAN REGRESS—CHILDREN CAN'T

I have heard parents and clinicians say that a child three or four years old is regressing. What this means to me is that the parents or clinicians are regressing. Children can't regress—they're too young. They can only act like the children they are. During infancy and early childhood, age is less linear and more circular. In most indigenous cultures, it is not unusual for a four-year-old who is watching his younger sibling nursing from his mother's breast to come over and take the other breast for a few moments.

A Western pediatrician would say that the child is regressing. I would say that the child is a child who still needs to test his or her mother's affection and wants to know that the newborn has not replaced his four-year-old self.

I have also heard that so-called temper tantrums are a sign of a child's regression. This is ridiculous. These children are simply trying to release pent-up anger and frustration, which is a healthy thing to do in most situations, especially in the safety of one's home. But if the parent interrupts or shames the child for shaking, crying, or yelling, it is probably because they were not allowed this normal behavior when they themselves were children.

Jill is one among hundreds of people whom I have worked with over the years who continually had her emotional releases (temper tantrums) interrupted by her parents. In fact, she was verbally, emotionally, and physically abused by her father both when she was very young and throughout her adolescence. While she was telling the workshop participants and me about the abuse, her body trembled. I asked her if she would like to lie down on the floor, which was padded with thick pillows and mats.

Jill started crying. "Could I?" she whispered. She lay down, and my assistants and I surrounded her for her protection. She continued sobbing. Her arms went akimbo, and she began thrusting her tightly balled-up fists into the pillows while she yelled and screamed. Then her legs went up and down on the thick mat. "I just wanted to scream. They wouldn't let me scream and yell. They always wanted me to be seen and not heard. Well, I'm here, I'm here, I'm here." She kept this up for about ten minutes. When she finished, she started laughing. "That felt so good, and it was so much fun. I didn't get hurt, and I didn't hurt anybody. My body feels so much lighter and looser. I may try that again sometime."

One thing that regressed parents do to their children is to try and make them grow up faster than they should. I would say that roughly half of all the people whom I have worked with over the last twenty years have had to consciously regress back to their childhood in order to deal with the trauma of having that childhood taken from them prematurely.

Andy was one of many clients who can remember being constantly told to "grow up" when he was only three years old.

Every time Angela's father left the house for the day, he would say to her, "Now you're a big girl. You take care of your mother." Angela remembers being five and hearing this.

Sharon was the oldest of five—three boys and two girls. Her father had died, and her mother worked full time to support the family. She would leave Sharon in charge of her siblings when Sharon was eight. Today her brothers and sisters still call her "Little Mamma."

Kevin recalls hearing his father say, "If you don't act your age, I'm not going to take you with me." Kevin was told this from the time he was four until he graduated from high school.

Most children have to grow up too fast. This is one of the main reasons regression occurs so often. During our short childhoods, many of us never got a chance to act, speak, or even think like kids. As adults, we unconsciously compensate by returning to childhood in as many ways as we can. We eat too much sugar because we couldn't have it as children. We play too much when we need to be working because, like me, many people had to work most of their childhood. My dad put me to work in his machine shop at age nine after school. Until I was seventeen, I worked on weekends and all of my summer vacations. If you think he was right, you are probably regressing because you too were made to work as a child.

Children surely can push the right buttons to make their parents go into a regression faster than lightning, but the bottom line is that they are just children. They are *supposed* to act like children, not like the adults that their parents may need them to be.

## PUNISHMENT VERSUS DISCIPLINE

A few years ago I was invited to return to Alabama and give the keynote address at the Alabama governor's conference on alcoholism and drug addiction. I was honored, to say the least, and excited since I had presented in nearly every state except the one I called home. I planned to give what I considered my best talk to impress my fellow Alabamians and, I hoped, be invited back in the future. On the morning I was to give my presentation, I was reading the Montgomery newspaper and saw an article about the young man who received a caning in Singapore for defacing a car. The writer was completely in support of such action and went on to laud the Montgomery school district for being one of the few school systems to keep corporal punishment. The article went on to describe how different-size paddles were used, depending on the grade level of the child. Elementary schools could only use a certain thickness. Junior high could be a little thicker, and high school was thicker still. I was sad and outraged that this was something that Alabama was proud of and was encouraging other states to emulate. After I read this article, I knew in my heart that I could not give the talk that I had planned.

At the conference, I began by saying, "If we want to reduce alcoholism and drug addiction, we must stop beating our children. How else can they numb the pain of abuse?"

The audience was not pleased. Out of eight hundred people, five hundred had left by intermission. During the break, a well-known Montgomery psychologist came up to me and said that he had used a belt and a board on his children, and that they were very "well adjusted." He said that I was completely wrong and then summarily left the conference.

At the end of my two-hour talk, only two hundred people remained. One principal of a middle school came up to me and said, "I have paddled kids for over twenty-five years. After this talk, I'm going to go to my office and burn that board."

An African-American woman in her late seventies came up and whispered in my ear, "Those people who left couldn't stand the heat because they knew you were right. I know it's wrong to hit children, and so do they. They just couldn't stand to hear it because they got hit when they were children. You keep saying what you're saying, and someday we'll come out of the dark ages. I've been a schoolteacher all my life, and I've seen what hitting does to kids. It's wrong." I never got invited back to the governor's conference.

Experts in the field of child psychology use the words *discipline* and *punishment* interchangeably, but they are two different things. Punishment is the act and behavior of a regressed man or woman. The *American Heritage Dictionary* defines *punishment* as "a penalty for wrongdoing" and as "rough handling; mistreatment." A regressed person handles their children roughly when punishing them. Out of the thousands of people with whom I have worked over the last twenty years, many clearly needed to do deep emotional release work around having been punished by parents, principals, coaches, military commanders, bosses, and spouses.

Punishment takes very little time and no forethought. It is capricious and very often malicious. Because it is so quick to execute, it catches the child off guard and doesn't give him or her time to mount a defense or to escape. Punishment is after the fact. There is no forethought, and therefore the consequences cannot be spelled out and a choice cannot be made.

Suppose little Timmy leaves his tricycle in the driveway. When his father gets home tired, stressed, and maybe hungry, he goes into his son's room and whips him. The father tells Timmy he can't ride his tricycle for a week until he learns to take better care of it. This kind of sudden, violent behavior leaves boys and girls wondering when their world will next be turned topsy-turvy, when they will receive their next whipping, scolding, or withholding. For Timmy's father, it was a quick release. In his regressed state, he saw it as "reasonable punishment." After all, tricycles cost money. He was trying to teach his three-year-old how to be responsible with his possessions. At least, that's what he thought he was doing.

The reason parents act in this way is because that's what they themselves were taught. They are trying to teach something to their children in good faith. But punishment doesn't teach. It creates anger, hostility, and resentment, and it communicates to children that they have no control over their bodies, brains, or souls. Every time James wet the bed when he was six, his father would make him sleep in their barn. James's father thought this punishment would break James of the "bad habit" by making it very uncomfortable for him. But he was wrong. James wet the bed until he was thirteen.

When his counselor at school began talking to him about his

poor grades, James said, "This makes my dad so mad, it's the only way I can get even with him for making me sleep in that damn cold barn because I wet my bed at night." The counselor was amazed and called his parents in for a consultation. Afterward James started seeing a therapist and got to some of the issues that were disturbing him the most. Soon the bed-wetting stopped. But thirty years later at my workshop, James was still angry for being punished that way and for the humiliation that went along with it.

In contrast to punishment, discipline takes time, forethought, follow-through, and most of all maturity. The *American Heritage Dictionary* defines *discipline* as "training expected to produce a specific character or pattern of behavior, and to obtain order." But I must tell you that the dictionary uses the word *punishment* or *punish* several times in its definitions, just as if the words were interchangeable.

Let's take the first definition, "training," since it's the correct one. Discipline takes place before the behavior, not after. Discipline trains the child to make conscious choices and decisions because Mom and Dad have clearly stated what the consequences of her behaviors will be before she does them. When she was in her early teens, my stepdaughter, Kate, came in thirty minutes late one evening. As she walked through the door, she shrugged and said, "I guess I'm grounded," and proceeded to her bedroom. I knocked and went in.

"Kate, did I tell you what the consequences would be if you were late?"

She looked at me as if this were a trick question. "No, you didn't."

"Well, that's my job as a parent. I forgot to tell you the consequences, so you are not going to be grounded. Now, tomorrow night if you are late, you will be grounded for the weekend. Good night." I knew she had a sleepover planned for the weekend, so I gave her the ability to choose. She could come home late again and lose her weekend with her friends, or she could be on time and enjoy her weekend.

Discipline requires adult consciousness, maturity, and lots of forethought. If the adult is tired and stressed, as most of us are these days, we may have only a few TMMs (temporary moments of maturity) per month. Hopefully, we can save a few to use for our children's sake.

Discipline reduces the inherent chaos in child rearing. Punishment increases the turmoil and confuses the child about the capriciousness of the world and the parents' love: "If I'm good, I won't get hit, slapped, rejected, or sent away to boarding school." But if a child is not told what is expected of her beforehand, sooner or later she is going to slip up and be "bad." Then she will be punished.

Bottom line—adults discipline their children and teach them healthy choice-making and responsibility. Regressed men and women punish their children, thereby teaching them that the world is a harsh and cruel place. In fact, they often inadvertently perpetuate negative behaviors by punishing their children. Simply put, punishment is child abuse. Disciplining children creates healthier, calmer, caring, and more considerate adults. Jane Nelson, Roslyn Duffy, and Cheryl Erwin say, in *Positive Discipline: The First Three Years*, "If you are screaming, yelling, or lecturing, stop. If you are spanking, stop. If you are trying to gain compliance through threats, stop. All of these methods are disrespectful and encourage doubt, shame, and guilt—now and in the future. Ultimately punishment creates more misbehavior."

If you were brought up in a religious home, you might argue,

"What about sparing the rod and spoiling the child?" Unfortunately, most clergymen have misinterpreted this passage. The rod in question was a long stick with a curved hook on the end. It was, and still is, used for pulling sheep out of thorns and away from precarious places. It was not used to beat the sheep for falling into briars and bushes. It is the same nurturing rod that is referred to in the phrase, "Thy rod and thy staff, they comfort me" in the Twenty-third Psalm. You should also know that in the Old Testament there is another passage that says, "When I was a child I thought as a child . . . and when I became a man, I put away childish things."

## COMPASSIONATE SYMPATHY FOR YOUNG CHILDREN

You might recall that in chapter 3 I explained the difference between sympathy and empathy. Sympathy means "I feel what you feel," while empathy means "I understand what you're going through because I've been through similar situations myself." Mature adults do not feel what other mature adults are feeling; nor do they feel what regressed men and women are feeling. If they do, then they themselves are regressing. But it *is* important and appropriate for adults to feel sympathy for children. If an adult is incapable of feeling what children, especially their own, are feeling, this is a red flag that they are regressing.

When a child is hungry, a caring, responsible adult will feel that child's discomfort and do something to alleviate it. A mature adult who sees a child in pain (physical or emotional) will take steps to comfort the child by first sensing or feeling the child's pain. In other words, he will show sympathy for the child. If possible, he will change that child's circumstances or surroundings, or provide her with comfort in the form of food, shelter, nurturing, touching, holding, rocking—anything that it takes to soothe the child.

If the so-called adult does not feel the child's discomfort in his own body, then this sets the stage for neglect and abuse. If a parent cannot feel the hunger in a child's belly, then the child will probably go unfed. But if the adult feels what the child feels, then he *must* do whatever is necessary to reduce not only the discomfort in the child's precious body but the discomfort the adult feels as well. When a caring adult sees pictures of starving children in Africa or elsewhere, she will be racked with pain and hopefully feel so much discomfort that she will be moved to donate the fifty cents a day that will nourish that child. In our hurried, worried, stressed society, it takes time to feel another's pain and even more time to do something constructive about it. Regressed men and women rationalize that it's not their job to feed hungry or clothe naked children. Adults know they cannot eradicate hunger, but that they can at least not add to it. They can perform some "random acts of kindness" to help those who are less fortunate.

## PRACTICING EMPATHY WITH OLDER CHILDREN

Child psychologists disagree about what age our sympathy for children should begin to diminish and be replaced by an empathy that still allows us to compassionately witness their feelings. Some say it should happen as early as four to six years of age. Others say much later. It has been my experience that, depending on a child's maturity level, parents should begin detaching from the child's feelings by the time she has reached the age of ten or eleven. If they have not done so by the time she is twelve or thirteen, there will be much discomfort and dysfunction in the household.

Working with adolescents for many years has taught me that thirteen-year-olds do not want their parents to "feel" what they feel. They are trying to separate from their parents and become autonomous human beings in their own right. If their parents are still feeling their pain at that age, it often causes the growing youths to act out in ways that make their parents feel bad, guilty, insignificant, or unnecessary.

By the time a child has reached puberty, she should be learning to "own" her feelings. That means identifying those feelings and articulating them. If the parents or primary caregivers are enmeshed with her, then they will find it difficult to separate what they themselves are feeling from what the young person is feeling.

Martha is an adult whose mother has not detached from her in a healthy way. To this day, her mother still tells her, "When you are sad, I feel sad for you." Martha shared this in the group at my last seminar. She went on to say, "For God's sake, I'm forty-one years old. And not only do I not know what I feel half the time, I feel like some of my mother's feelings are in my body, and I don't like that. It's hard enough to feel what I feel, let alone separate her feelings from mine."

If you are a parent, you may think that once your child is born, you will always feel what he feels. That is because our society does not have rituals and ceremonies that clearly mark the end of childhood and the beginning of adulthood. In many indigenous cultures, the separation between those two states of being is honored in ritual, and the whole village witnesses and supports the end of childhood and the beginning of a new adult life. In the Mayan villages of Guatemala, when a boy successfully completes his initiation into manhood, he returns with a new name and addresses his "former" parents by a new name as well.

The old adage, "If you will feel my feelings for me, then why should I feel them?" shows great wisdom. I don't know how many men and women I have worked with over the last two decades who have said something to me like "My husband carries both my anger and his" or "My wife is sad enough for the both of us." These men and women were, more often than not, raised in families that taught them that it is a noble and self-sacrificing thing to feel someone else's feelings. Yet all of these people have experienced anger, frustration, or resentment at having carried another's feelings or at having their own feelings felt by their parents throughout childhood, adolescence, and even middle age.

If parents do not model this natural progression from feeling to empathizing, they will teach their children to do the same with their own children. In other words, a thirty-five-year-old father should not "feel" his adolescent boy's awkwardness, clumsiness, or shyness. But having gone through that hard and difficult stage himself, he probably can empathize with his son.

Should he turn to his son, however, and say, "I know how you feel," the son would be correct to look at him and say, "No way. You can't know how I feel. These feelings are mine—not yours."

## LETTING YOUR ADULT CHILDREN GO

There is an old saying that goes, "Parents who can't let go of their children raise children who can't let go of their parents."

Let's be clear about what *letting go* means. It does not mean you stop caring or loving the person or being concerned for her.

It means that you gradually let go and begin to view her as an adult, then behave accordingly. Just as you wouldn't interfere in matters that didn't concern you with fellow adults, you extend the same courtesy and respect to your adult children. You stop talking to them like kids and engage them as mature thinking adults.

I have heard hundreds of mothers say, "But you don't understand. They'll always be my little boy or girl. That's just the way a mother feels."

Some mothers feel this way because, like Jackie, they put all their time, energy, and attention into the art of mothering. Jackie was good at it, but she didn't develop any other interests, hobbies, or skills. Thus, when her children were grown, she didn't have anything or anybody to turn her attention toward. Now she calls her adult children every day, meddles in their affairs, and gives them unsolicited advice. Two of her adult children, Ernie and Joe, were in my last workshop; I asked them to pretend that their mother was in an empty chair. Both men yelled at her to let them go, to let them grow up, and to get a life of her own. At the end of the session, they said that they loved her and always would, but they needed her to *let them go*. Ernie is forty, and Joe is forty-eight.

When is it time to let your children go? Developmentally, a parent starts separating from a child at around the age of two. Then little by little the child sees himself as a separate human being. By adolescence, he begins to have a clearly defined sense of self. By the late teens and early twenties, the letting-go process should be firmly in place.

When men and women tell me their parents are still "running" their lives, they are angry, bitter, and resentful. What I do is have them sit in a chair and close their eyes. I have them take full deep breaths. Then I tell them, "The hands you are going to take hold of are your father's [or mother's] hands." I ask them to reach out. Usually, by this time they have started to weep. I say, "I want you to see how it feels to say these words: 'Good-bye, Mom [Dad]. It's time to let you go. I've got to let you go and get on with my life.'"

When they say this, I keep holding on to their hands, showing them viscerally that their parent will not let go, because this is usually the case. At this point the participant begins to struggle and sometimes even gets angry, saying, "You have to let me go. I'm a grown man [or woman]."

Then I usually say something like "Maybe there's one or two things you need to say to Mom [or Dad] before you can really let her go."

Most often the person says to the imagined parent, "I never really had you in the first place" or "It's so hard to let you go" or "Why can't you let me go and get on with your own life?" Very often just before they drop my hands, they'll say, "I love you."

It is my belief that one of the most loving things that parents and adult children can do for each other is to let each other go with love. Sometimes when the ties are binding us to the point of choking us, love loosens those ties, and sometimes it is grief or anger that helps us to let go and get on with being adults.

One of the most loving things you can do for your parents and children and partners is to learn that letting go doesn't mean never seeing them again. It just means letting go of the roles, patterns, and behaviors that no longer work.

## CHAPTER 8

## THE GRACE OF REGRESSION

If the prospect of letting go does little to encourage you, then perhaps grace will be more comforting. That is, unless you are uncomfortable with the word *grace* because of leftover or unresolved feelings about religion, church, or spiritual abuse—in which case, the very word *grace* may send you hurtling back in time. If so, then let me give you another word that you might use in its place. Even though I'll continue to use *grace*, you just replace it with the word *gift*.

I use the word *grace* very intentionally for several reasons. First, *grace* is not something that we cannot bestow on ourselves. The gift of *grace* is given by God, Universe, Spirit, One, the Almighty, the Goddess or God within—whatever you choose to call your Higher Power.

Regression is not a problem that can be fixed once and for all—go to a regression workshop, read the book, and *presto chango,* you will never regress again. Regression is part of the human condition. You and I will always regress from time to time, sometimes more than others, sometimes less. But there is grace in regression, because once we understand that we are engaged in a continual, deepening process of growing and maturing spiritually and emotionally, we can become more patient with ourselves and with others. The more I realize that I am in process, and not some finished product coming off the human assembly line, the more I can settle into life with less anxiety and more optimism.

The second reason there is grace in regression is that every time I regress, I am given one more opportunity to heal an old trauma, hurt, slight, grievance, or resentment, or to take care of old unfinished business. Life gives us these opportunities over and over again.

## CHOICES

All human beings are born with free will. We can choose to stay in our trances, or we can choose to become conscious of when we are regressing—to identify that state and make a commitment to heal and grow ourselves up. It's our choice. Some people will consciously choose to do the work necessary to keep themselves in an adult place as much of the time as possible. Others either aren't ready or have decided that this material doesn't apply to *them*—although their ex-husband or wife sure could use it.

You can choose to use this material in many ways. You can use it to catch yourself before you go into a regression, or at least to catch yourself sooner than you did before. And you can learn, with time, patience, and practice, to come out of your regression faster.

If you want to avoid regressing, it is wise to minimize the amount of time you spend with people who do not support you, or who shame, criticize, blame, teach, preach, judge, or analyze you. You can instead choose to search for others who are as committed as you are to staying adult as much as possible. And you can be forgiving and compassionate when they fail.

The fact that you regress does not mean that you are a failure. You can choose to consciously recognize it as the great teacher it is and learn from it. An adult is someone who acknowledges that it is her failures that have gotten her to where she is now. It is failure that makes you appreciate your own successes and the successes of others. Your mistakes make you part of the human race and give you more to talk about than your victories. You can, when you are in an adult place, relate to Antonio Machado's lines:

> *Last night, as I was sleeping,*
> *I dreamt—marvellous error!—*
> *that I had a beehive*
> *here inside my heart.*
> *And the golden bees*
> *were making white cones*
> *and sweet honey*
> *from my old failures.*

Antonio Machado, "Last Night" (translated by Robert Bly)

I once heard someone ask for the definition of *adult*. I can't remember where I was, or who the speaker was who answered the question, but I'll never forget the answer: "Adult means choice."

As children, most of us had little or no say in most matters. My generation was taught that children should be seen and not heard. We were told to "do as I say, not as I do." We didn't have a "vote" in family matters because we were "just children."

Picture this scenario if you will. Five-year-old Jerry has just received his umpteenth whipping or scolding. He turns to his parents and says, "You know, Mom and Dad, I choose not to be abused anymore. I'll be taking the car keys, withdrawing some money from our joint account, and moving to Florida to live with Grandma and Grandpa. When you both start acting like adults, give me a call, and we'll discuss the conditions of my return. We'll see if we can settle on a mutual arrangement where you two stay adult as much of the time as possible, and I'll be a kid who learns how to make healthy choices by being disciplined instead of punished. We'll negotiate how you will set healthy boundaries so I can learn to do the same. For now, I'll be seeing you. Don't forget to write. And don't forget to read John Lee's book on regression. I'm too young, but you're not."

As children, we did not have the choice of laying down the law for our frequently regressing parents. But as adults we can certainly choose to draw our boundaries and express our needs in all of our relationships as adults—not only with our parents, but also with our spouses, friends, colleagues, and acquaintances.

## WE CAN REGRESS AND REGRET IT

Take a deep breath, then another, and another, until you feel relaxed. Close your eyes, and picture at least one time when you regressed so thoroughly and completely that it cost you something that you have regretted your entire life.

Okay. What did you come up with? When I do this exercise, I find that what I regret more than anything is regressing with the people I love the most. But here's the real kicker: Regret is a symptom of regression. If an adult regrets something that he has done, but then doesn't make it right with the person he has hurt, then he is still regressed. He is not making true amends.

When I was twelve or thirteen, my buddy and I would go to Kmart. I'd flirt with the pretty seventeen-year-old girl working in the music section. I'd get her to open the case that held those precious eight-track tape cassettes, and then while I distracted her by joking and carrying on, my friend would start stuffing tapes into his pants. We stopped when his pants were full—and pants were pretty big in those days. Now why do I regret this? For two reasons. One, I was not a child. I knew this was wrong, but I had regressed to an infantile place where there is no right or wrong, just pleasure and pain. My friend and I got extreme pleasure and profit from selling those tapes to our other friends. The second reason for regret is that I don't know where that young woman is and thus will never be able to give her an adult apology for putting her at risk of losing her job. That Kmart went out of business more than twenty years ago. I guess I could write a letter to the national headquarters, but I don't remember whether we stole ten tapes, twenty tapes, or three dozen. If I could, I would give them all back.

What I'm trying to say is that not all regrets can be remedied. In fact, by the time you reach my age, you won't even be able to remember most of them. But for the ones that you can recall—and if making amends will not do further harm—you should probably take the time and energy to write or phone an apology. Did you regress with your children? It's never too late to apologize. Call them and tell them just how deeply sorry you are. Stay in your adult place, which means not expecting anything from them. In the heat of anger, rage, or regression, did you divorce someone whom you really loved? Write her a letter and make amends. So what if she is happily married? As long as you are sure it won't damage her new marriage, you can turn your regret into a mistake. Forgive yourself, and move on with your life.

Don't go to your grave regretting that you never made that call or wrote that letter.

## THE DETOUR METHOD

I hope by now you have a thorough understanding of what emotional regression is, what causes it, and how to avoid it. I hope you realize that it is always going to be a part of your life. But if you can learn to utilize the following techniques and tools, I promise you that you will be doing everyone, including yourself, a big favor. I'll make an even bigger promise: You will be able to improve, enhance, and even save relationships that are important to you.

In the 1940s and 1950s, our culture considered it inappropriate for people to tell anyone how they were feeling, hurting, or healing, or what they needed or wanted. In the 1960s, psychologists and social revolutionaries encouraged us to "let it all hang out," to engage in "straight talk" to learn to "confront others" or "call people on their shit," and to be "rigorously honest" or "radically truthful." This was a huge step forward for mankind—but also in some ways a giant leap into regression. By tacking our little self to someone who can be empathetic and objective, we save ourselves and others a great deal of time and energy.

Straight talk might be a direct line to a problem, but it does not help us achieve closer connection and deeper intimacy. It does not necessarily help us hear another person or be heard. One reason it misses the mark is that the people who are talking straight are more often than not regressed, and regressed people do not think clearly. Therefore, what comes out of their mouths is not very clear. This is why so many of us have had marathon processing sessions that took hours instead of minutes, or weeks instead of days.

At my Regression Intensives, one of the first things I say is this: "If I say or don't say something, or do or don't do something, that makes you so upset that you can hardly sit in your seat or hear what I say—if anything makes you dissociate or want to leave—I ask you to go to one of my senior staff. Take them aside, and tell them what you're feeling and thinking. If after you have done so, you still want to speak with me, I'll be happy to make time to listen. But I won't meet with you until you've met with them first."

After experiencing thousands of hours of seminars and intensives, I have learned that when someone comes up to me afterward wanting to "talk," what they want is not about me. Instead, something said that day has triggered a memory from their past. For that reason, I do not enable their regression. I choose not to allow them to use me to dump out pent-up, stored-up, repressed feelings from the past. Instead, I encourage them to experience a Conscious Regression with a member of my staff and discover what I said or did that triggered the memory. In other words, instead of letting everyone bring their past to me, I ask them to take a detour. And if they still feel that they must talk to me afterward, I can usually still hear them out without going into a regression myself.

At my last intensive, a young man came up to me and said, "We need to talk."

"We" is a red flag. I said, "Have you talked to one of my staff yet about what's going on?"

"No. I'm sure it's about me and you."

He looked very anxious and intense. I said, "I really need you to talk to Vijay Director or Connie Burns or Karen Blicher before we talk." He agreed and went outside with Vijay, a senior trainer and facilitator.

After about thirty minutes, they came back into the main group. The young man had clearly been crying, and his face was much more relaxed. I asked him if he still needed to talk with me.

He smiled. "I realized I went into a huge regression and made you into my father," he said. "I told Vijay that I had been here for a full day and that you had not once made eye contact with me, and that I thought you were avoiding me. Vijay said, 'Take this towel and twist it and say, "Look at me, see me," to the person you are really angry with.' He made me do this over and over again until I realized who I really wished had seen me. Of course, it was my father. He was almost always gone, and when he was home, he tended to avoid me and busy himself with anything but me. That really hurt me and made me angry. My dad never really saw me."

I went over and put my arm around him, with his permission, and said, "Do you feel heard and seen now?"

He looked right into my eyes. "Yeah, you're not my dad."

The Detour Method is designed to help people avoid dumping "stuff" from the past onto an innocent person in the present. It is my experience that not using the Detour Method is a leading cause of divorce, breakups, misunderstandings, miscommunication, and the premature termination of friendships, working relationships, and even parent-child relationships. Not taking a detour can take you so off track that you never really get back on it.

If your body has not had its say, if your emotions have been held in for too long, then don't dump on the wrong person just because they happen to be close to you. Go to a third party—an objective person who will hear you out and not be pulled into your regression. Find someone who will allow you to say, do, or feel what you needed to say, do, or feel many years ago. With the help of this third party, you can regain your adult state. Only then should you go and tell your loved one what you need.

Who is this third party? Anybody who can really listen to you and give you attention, time, touch, and empathy. This third party could be a friend, a safe person, a therapist, or someone in a support group. If you can't find someone like that, then tell your feelings to a lake, a mountain, or an oak tree. Scream your feelings to your Higher Power. Your Higher Power can take it. But do not risk your present relationship by dumping your stuff onto them. Trust me, they have enough stuff of their own and don't need yours or mine.

Here is a classic example of a couple who drove straight past a sign that was blaring, "Take a detour!" Lisa is a petite woman who lives in Arizona. She and her husband, Carl, told me about a seemingly insignificant event that almost landed them in divorce court. Carl is a tall, wiry man who works for the telephone company. Like me, he's from the South, where most cities grew because the railroad ran through them. Remember the movie and book *Fried Green Tomatoes*? Kids would constantly play "chicken" with the trains, first on foot, then later by car. Carl and I had done both in our youth.

One day Carl and Lisa were out house hunting. They were ready to move out of their rented apartment and put down roots. But first they had to find a suitable house. Brad wanted an older home so that he could restore it and perhaps sell it later to make a profit. He had done this several times before and enjoyed fixing things up. Lisa, on the other hand, had never lived in an older home. She liked things to be new. She had always lived in new houses while growing up, and in new apartments when she was single.

The house issue set them off, and while they were driving around looking at houses, they both regressed into the past and into the way they had been raised. They were not in the present. As they drove through an old southern town, they came upon a railroad crossing. The bells started ringing, and the crossing arms began to fold down.

Carl said later, "I looked both directions and couldn't see a thing coming. So I just went around the barrier and kept on going. You would have thought I had killed someone because Lisa went ballistic. She said, 'I can't believe you did that. You broke the law. Why didn't you wait? You could have gotten us killed!'

"She went on and on, until I finally yelled at her to stop yelling at me. I told her, 'I just went around a train stop. Stop talking to me like a child. Don't ever use that tone of voice with me again!' Well, we must have argued about that incident for two hours, and we ended up not sleeping together that night and not talking the next day. I didn't know what the hell was going on. Finally, I remembered your tape, *The Rhythm of Closeness*, and played it on my way to work. When I got to work, I called a good friend and told him what had happened. By the end of the conversation, I realized that when I was a little boy, my mother would always tell my father how to drive. She would scold him and talk down to him as if he were a child. I had always wanted him to make her stop, but he just kept taking it year after year. Hell, she still tells him how to drive.

"So when Lisa yelled at me for going through the train crossing, I became the kid in the backseat watching his mother demean his father. Yesterday I became the father who finally stood up for himself, but to do so I had to turn Lisa into my mother. After the phone call, I called Lisa and apologized for turning her into my mother."

It turned out that Lisa had done her own growing up in the meantime. She realized that she had lost her adultness in that situation because her father, who was an alcoholic, used to drive when he got drunk and insult and take crazy risks with her, her mother, and her two brothers. "I hated seeing Mother disrespected like that," Lisa said as she wept. "I felt Carl was acting like my father, disrespecting me by not asking me if it was okay for us to go around the signal. I would at least have wanted to know what he was going to do before he did it. So I became my mom who was always yelling and screaming at my dad, and Carl just disappeared."

For Carl, the regression was a very serious one. "For a day or two, I thought, 'Man, have I married my mother again?' For a while I was so regressed that I was even thinking, 'I'm getting out of this before we buy a house.'" That's how far this kind of regression can escalate.

## WALKING THROUGH THE DETOUR METHOD STEP BY STEP

The Detour Method takes us where we really want to go: into the arena of better communication, closer connection, and deeper intimacy. The Detour Method allows a person to be heard and feel heard. It teaches us how to listen.

If you feel that something you heard, saw, or felt is causing you to regress, practice the Detour Method. First take a few deep breaths. Then check out your body and identify the signals it is giving you. Is there a knot in your stomach? Has your mouth gone dry? Are your extremities cold, is your heart beating faster, and did your neck and chest tighten? Are you experiencing shortness of breath? If the answer is yes to any of these questions, then it's time to take the detour.

The second step is to either call or visit someone whom you trust and feel safe with. Tell them what happened and what you are feeling right then and there. This person should be able to remain objective, even if she knows the person who has triggered this regression in you. She does not need to be a trained therapist, and sometimes it is even better if she is not. She needs only to be a nonanxious person who feels safe and attentive. She should also make sure that what she is hearing is not triggering something in her, making her go into a regression herself.

Since the person who triggered you is not present and cannot hear you, it is fair and appropriate for you to say anything you need to say any way that you want to say it. What the listener has to do after you get out all your feelings is to ask a question, phrasing it in one of several ways. (You have made her aware of these questions ahead of time, by telling her "Once I have told you my problem, this is what I will want you to ask me.")

- "DO YOU RECALL ANY OTHER PEOPLE WHO DID THIS SAME THING TO YOU?"
- "WHEN WAS THE FIRST TIME YOU REMEMBER FEELING THIS WAY? WERE THERE OTHER TIMES?"
- "WHO ELSE IN YOUR PAST TREATED YOU THIS WAY?"

You answer these questions. Then the listener might say something like "What did you really want to say or do to that person back then, if you could have said or done it without getting hurt?"

At this point, you will usually cry, get angry, or do both. Say what you have always wanted to say. If that is not enough, then the listener can suggest that you release your emotions further. You can either twist a towel, beat a pillow, or scream out words like "Stop," "No more," "Enough," "Go away," "Leave me alone," "Don't treat me this way," "I'm leaving," or "I just wanted you to love me." In other words, say and feel whatever has previously gone unspoken or unfelt.

The next thing the listener might do is to simply say, "Now how are you feeling?" or "Who else needs to be told how you felt?"

If you find yourself breathing a deep sigh of relief, the chances are good that you have grown yourself back up. All you need to do now, from an adult place, is thank the listener who has given you such good attention. Then decide what, if anything, you need to say to the person that triggered the regression in the first place. If you need to go and apologize, do so.

It has been my experience that we can learn to perceive incidents or comments that set us off as gifts. They can provide us with an opportunity to go back into our bodies and our pasts and heal something that had been hurting us for a long time. If you have something left to say to the person who originally triggered your regression, you can probably say it in five or ten minutes. The person will almost certainly not become defensive or put off because you are communicating from an adult place, speaking appropriately.

What if you have no listener to accompany you on your detour? Then you have to take the detour alone. If you are not too far regressed, you can ask yourself the same questions that a good empathic listener would ask: "Who does he (or she) remind me of from my past? When did something like this happen in my past?" Take a piece of paper, and write down your answers. If writing doesn't work for you, scream out the answers. Yell out what you would have liked to say to that person from your past. A good place to do this type of emotional release is in the woods, where no one is around. Trees, rocks, and clouds love to listen.

One very important thing to remember when employing the Detour Method is to let the person who triggered your regression know that you are taking a time-out. If possible, let him know how much downtime you will need. If in that time period you still have not grown yourself back up, be kind enough and adult enough to let him know that you need more time.

Telling the triggering person that you are taking a time-out, even if you do it in a completely appropriate manner, may trigger that person to go into their own regression. She may feel abandoned or unimportant, ways she felt as a child. Or he may accuse you of avoiding the issue. These are signals that he may be regressing into his own past.

Whatever effect your time-out has on the triggering person is not your primary concern. If you fail to continue the detour, you will be essentially robbing yourself of your opportunity to look at, feel, and maybe heal an old wound. This is the very point in the Detour Method where there is the greatest potential for getting stuck. So your priority should be to take care of yourself and grow yourself back up as soon as possible, so that you can be present and attentive to your wife, husband, lover, children, parents, friend, boss, or employee.

My wife, Susan, and I are a good example of moving forward. I am writing this chapter at our little cottage in Mentone, in the mountains of northern Alabama. I come here often to write or just to unwind. Sometimes Susan comes with me, but not this time.

I was supposed to be back home in Marietta today, but I decided to stay a day longer because I am really on a roll. I miss Susan very much, and she misses me. But I have been writing all morning, have really enjoyed it, and have gotten quite a bit done. When she called, I told her I needed to keep going while the creative juices were flowing. She said, "Then, honey, if you need to stay another day, I totally support you to do so. I understand and I'll be fine."

I'm telling you this because three years ago when I would tell her that I needed to go to the cottage for a few days, she would look as if I had told her that I was leaving her for good. She would get very sad and blue, and that would throw me into my own regression. I'd start thinking, *Maybe I should just stay here with her. That way she won't have to feel what she's feeling.* In other words, *I'll take care of her at the expense of what I need.*

Luckily, I had experienced enough support, guidance, therapy, and recovery that I did not feel I had to rescue her. I simply allowed her to feel whatever she needed to feel. Still, until a year ago, all the way to the cottage I would be thinking about turning that car around and going back to her so she wouldn't have to feel what my absence was bringing up.

After three years, she doesn't feel abandoned anymore because she took her own detours and got the support and help she needed around her abandonment issues and her fear of being alone. And I don't regress and feel the need to rescue her nearly as often as I used to.

So if I had gone home today, it would have been because I had dropped my emotional boundaries and gone with her rhythms and needs instead of my own. Now don't get me wrong—there are times when we should compromise, and adults should be ready, willing, and able to do so at those times. But a conscious adult has learned to tell the difference between the two and has struck a healthy balance in his or her life and relationships.

## KEEPING GOOD EMOTIONAL BOUNDARIES AND STAYING ADULT

First off, what is a boundary? I don't know whether being from Alabama has anything to do with it, but I need to keep things very simple in my life in order to maintain some modicum of psychological health. To me, a boundary is simply a line that you can't step over unless I let you. A boundary is how far you can come toward me with words, actions, feelings, and touch.

On the other hand, a *limit*, which is essential to keeping good boundaries, describes how far I will go with my words, actions, feelings, and touch based on how I feel in the moment. Limits come into relationships by imposing consequences. In other words, if you defile my boundaries and push my limits, sooner or later I will announce the consequences and then follow through with them.

For example, I will not be called names—that is my boundary. I will not call you names—that is a limit. If you continue to call me names, I will have to leave until I feel that you will honor my limit and boundary—that is a consequence that I will follow through on. If, when I return, you persist in calling me names, I may have to remove myself for a longer period or even permanently—that is the ultimate consequence.

The sad thing about regression is that most people have not been taught how to build strong emotional boundaries, set limits, and create consequences they can follow through on. Therefore, they resort to building virtually impenetrable walls and barricades between themselves and others. They surround themselves with deep moats and fill them with crocodiles that are ready to chew off a limb or bite off a head.

Joseph, a client who was going through a huge transition in his life, came to see me for a private consultation. He was getting ready to quit a job he'd been working at for twenty years and go into a completely different line of work. He was switching from software development to opening his own music store.

Major life changes like this almost invariably make someone regress, so I asked Joseph to share one of his greatest fears surrounding the change.

"Well, the first fear that comes up is that I'll fail. The next fear is my fear of telling my father. I know he'll tell me I'm crazy for giving up the job I have for my dream of opening a store that sells musical instruments."

I asked him what he intended to do about telling his father.

"I don't think I'm going to be visiting my father for a while. He'll just put me down and shame me. So I'm going to wait about a year or two after I've done it and seen whether I'm a success before I tell him anything about it."

I asked Joseph, "When you think about telling your father about this change, how old do you feel?"

Without a moment's hesitation he answered, "Twelve or thirteen."

"And when you think about not seeing him for a year or two, how old do you feel?"

"The same age."

"Joseph, how old are you?"

"Fifty-three."

"Are you running away from home?"

He started weeping. After about ten minutes, I asked him if he would be willing to do a boundary-setting exercise with me. He said yes.

"I want you to pretend to be your father, and I'll pretend to be you," I said. "'Dad, I'm making a change in careers,'" I began. "'I'm excited about it and scared. I'd appreciate any support and encouragement you can give me.'"

Joseph slumped in the chair and smacked his hand against his forehead and said, "'What, are you crazy?'"

Before he could say anything else, I said, "'Dad, I will not be disparaged or demeaned.'"

Joseph looked at me with bewilderment. "Wow, you mean I could just say 'Stop. I won't be talked to this way'?"

"What do you think he would do if you did say something like that? What would happen if you set a boundary with your dad as to how you will allow him to talk to you?"

Joseph was silent for four or five minutes, and then he finally said, "The truth is, John, I haven't got a clue about what he would say or do because I've never said anything like that before. I usually just let him tear me down, and then I blow up and leave. That's the way it's been all my life."

If you are not used to setting boundaries, don't expect to do it perfectly the first time, and don't expect the people you're doing it with to readily appreciate your increasing emotional health. You and they may have a decades-long history of relating to each other in a predictable, patterned manner. But if you are willing to appropriately and consistently set boundaries in an adult manner, you will eventually see progress.

Adults are people who decide to make a conscious commitment to getting all the help, support, and safety they need. They take one brick at a time out of their walls so that they can replace those impenetrable walls with boundaries. They fill in their moats and remove their crocodiles one by one and replace them with healthy boundaries. They take down their barricades and barriers and replace them with limits.

While you are doing this, however, remember that moving too fast is one of the worst regressors there is. Being too quick to take down barriers can be detrimental to your emotional, mental, and physical health—people and institutions can harm you. Another pitfall to avoid is expecting yourself to set "perfect" boundaries all the time.

## ADULTS LEARN HOW TO LISTEN

Really listening to another person is difficult. Dozens of books have been written on active listening. Most women would trade a man's good looks for the ability to listen. Most men would trade just about anything to really be heard. Okay, that may be stretching it a bit, but men still want their partner to hear them.

If you want to really be heard by someone, and if you want to cultivate the art of listening to another person without letting their pain seep into your body, all you have to do is remember B&B—breath and boundaries. Most people, when they are in the presence of sadness, anger, pain, or trauma, tend to stop breathing full deep breaths and take in only minimal amounts of oxygen. This sets the stage for taking on the other person's emotions. Shallow breathing causes tension and stress, which increases the likelihood that the person listening will start regressing too. At that point, the listener will either start fixing, taking care of, making suggestions, analyzing, preaching, teaching, judging, or criticizing.

Full deep breaths allow the listener to relax and stay centered and detached. It conveys to the person speaking the nonverbal message that the listener is okay with what is being said and is fully present and attentive.

We've already discussed setting boundaries in detail. But I think it's important to mention a useful tool to help those who are just beginning to exchange walls for boundaries.

Try the following exercise: Close your eyes, and begin taking in full deep breaths through your nose and exhaling out of your mouth. Drop your jaw and relax. Get as comfortable as you can, and keep breathing. Now, picture yourself completely enclosed in a glass globe or an old bell jar. In this jar or globe you can see everything around you, and you can be seen. You can hear everything, and you can be heard by anyone.

Take a deep breath. Know that in this protected state, you can really see and listen to anyone. When the suffering person has finished speaking, you will feel just as fine, as safe, and as balanced as you did when she began sharing her emotions with you. That bell jar or globe is yours to access at all times. It is your boundary.

Another important strategy to keep from taking on another person's pain is to stay current with your own. Practice Conscious Regression on your own issues as often as you can. Think of your body as a vessel, and clean out that vessel as often as you can. Pour out all your pent-up anger, sadness, grief, fear, and loneliness. This exercise will take you far in increasing your ability to listen to others.

## HELPING OTHERS TO STAY GROWN UP BY STAYING GROWN UP YOURSELF

By breathing, setting firm boundaries, and keeping your own emotional life up to date and cleared out, you will be able to stay an adult much more of the time. If you do these things, those around you will automatically minimize their own regressions. The explanation for this phenomenon is both scientific and a little mystical. There is something about energy that neither the mystic nor the physicist completely understands. As Thaddeus Golas says in *The Lazy Man's Guide to Enlightenment*, any mass, including people, is either contracting or expanding, but it is never standing still. According to Einstein's theories of relativity and the laws of thermodynamics, energy is always in motion.

If I am breathing full deep breaths, expanding my lungs and my chest, and relaxing my muscles, all of this movement communicates expansion. When I take shallow breaths, squint, furrow my brow, become tense, and shut down emotionally, I am contracting.

We know that water seeks its own level. So if I can stay conscious enough to continually expand, I will draw people to me who will be naturally attracted to this kind of mature, adult energy. But remember that regression loves company. Once you start to contract, I must employ all my techniques for staying an expanded adult. If I don't, I will quickly begin to "sink" to your level. We've all had that "sinking feeling." On the other hand, if I can remain an adult, then you will eventually start expanding again and come back into your adulthood. Either that, or you'll leave and go seek someone who is as contracted and regressed as you are. Misery loves company, and everybody loves a winner.

## REGRESSION AS A TOOL FOR GROWTH

So you see, there is grace in regression. Regression, like anger or grief, is not a negative thing that one can cure, fix, or avoid. Handled in an appropriate way, it is a good thing. It gives us opportunity after opportunity to connect with the deepest parts of our selves, our memories, our emotions, or our Higher Power.

As I write this in my little cottage on the mountain, the wind is blowing the chimes outside my window, and I'm sitting by a stone fireplace. I look around and remember the day I finished moving in my things. A beautiful quilt that my grandmother's mother made for her is hanging on the wall. On the other wall is a quilt that my grandmother made for my mother, who gave it to me. I have an antique sewing machine from the early 1900s in one corner.

This place is so different from my office in Marietta, Georgia, which is filled with Native American artifacts and gifts from the many tribes I have worked with over the years. Everything in my office tends toward the masculine. But this house is full of the feminine, including little knickknacks that were left by the old couple that sold it to me and some of my own. When I bought this house and furnished it and fixed it up, I was in a deep regression. I didn't realize this until about a week or so later, when my mother came to visit. As she looked around, I asked her, "What does this house remind you of?"

Without a moment's hesitation, she said, "Your grandmother's house."

"Yeah, it's just like her old place. I didn't know how much I really loved her until I looked at how I'd decorated this place." I wept with sadness that I hadn't spent more time with her and with joy that, in my regressed state, I had connected with her wonderful spirit.

This is one of the things I am talking about when I speak of the grace of regression. Regression into the past can sometimes take us to a very good place indeed. Every time I come to my cabin, I feel so nurtured and relaxed. My regression gave me a little of my grandmother and a little bit of God. In the woods that surround this place, I can feel the presence of my grandfather Lee. He taught me how to appreciate nature, especially the rocks that jut out of the ground here and there for no apparent purpose. They remind me of him and all he taught me about Spirit.

So while it is sometimes painful for us to consciously regress, it will invariably bring us healing. While going into Trance Regression sometimes causes us and others pain, in time and with practice, we can learn to catch ourselves more quickly and come out more rapidly. Consciously regressing, and learning how to grow ourselves back up, can bring us many moments of ecstasy and joy. I thank God for regression, and I thank you for reading this far. I hope this book helps you or someone you know.

# CHAPTER 9

## NOTES ON REGRESSION
## FOR THERAPISTS AND OTHER
## HELPING PROFESSIONALS

*Effective therapists seem to follow this implicit hypothesis: If they are themselves in the presence of the patient, if they let their patient and themselves be, avoiding compulsions to silence, to reflection, to interpretation, to impersonal technique, and kindred character disorders, but instead striving to know their patient, involving themselves in his situation, and then responding to his utterances with their spontaneous selves, this fosters growth. In short, they love their patients.*

SIDNEY M. JOURARD, *The Transparent Self*

Many therapists and other helping professionals (like medical staff, police officers, lawyers, teachers, clergy, social workers, coaches, counselors, and so on) are constantly put in situations that make them regress. Some are aware that they are regressing, but most are not. Regression is one of the single greatest contributors to professional burnout. Countless people leave professions they love, not because they stop loving what they do or because they are ineffective at their jobs, but because they do not know how to actively treat their own tendencies to regress with the methods that I have described.

Last year I gave a seminar on regression to more than five hundred therapists and social workers. On their evaluation forms, the overwhelming majority said they had never heard regression discussed in this manner, and they wanted to know how to get further training in managing it. I was both flattered and confused. This is why I have included this special chapter on regression for those of us who are in helping professions.

## HOW TO REDUCE YOUR OWN REGRESSION WITH CLIENTS

Amy is a competent lawyer who has made a great living helping her clients move through the painful transition of divorce. She attended my workshop on regression last fall for the sole reason that she felt ready to give up her work for a profession that was a little less painful and stressful. As she talked, her small-framed body curled into a small ball on her chair, and she said to the group about her work, "I know that I help people, but I just don't think I can do it anymore. I'm finding that I can't sleep well at night, I've lost a lot of weight, and I just don't have the energy I once had." She started to cry.

I asked her what she was feeling, and she replied, "I'm sad, just terribly sad all the time." She wept profoundly for several minutes. Finally, I asked her if she was married. "No, not anymore. My husband and I were married for fifteen years. I thought it was a pretty good marriage until the day he asked for the divorce. It came out of the blue and really threw me."

"Amy, who helped you through that transition?"

She looked at me as if I had slapped her with a subpoena. "No one helped me. I just got through it somehow. I didn't even tell my parents until the papers had been signed. I was so ashamed that my marriage had failed. For the longest time, I didn't want anyone to know. I'm even embarrassed to be saying this in front of this group of strangers."

Amy and I worked on this issue several times during the four-day retreat. She released a tremendous amount of sadness and anger and worked very deeply on letting go of her shame. On the last day she told the group that she wasn't going to quit her work, but that when she got home, she was going to find a good therapist who offered ongoing group counseling for the recently divorced.

Amy had been helping everyone but herself. Every time she helped someone through his or her divorce, she would unconsciously feel resentful, angry, and sad that no one had helped her through hers. At the workshop, she was able to trace her shame at not being able to ask for help back to her father. His motto was "Keep family problems to yourself." He had drilled this philosophy into her since she was a little girl. During her divorce, she said, "I was a little girl who didn't really know what she was doing. I just needed the kind of help that I so readily gave to others."

Ruth is another example of classic burnout. A tall brunette in her early twenties, she works at a small day care center in New

York City. She loves children and hopes to have some of her own one day. Since she is working on her master's degree in psychology, her job at the day care center allows her to have a flexible schedule and enough money to manage. She was at the same workshop that Amy attended.

Ruth said that she understood what Amy was going through, but that her situation was different in some way that she couldn't quite figure out. I asked her what she liked the most about her work, and without a moment's hesitation, she said, "The children. They're so beautiful and precious." She then began to get very angry. Her face turned red, and she clenched both of her fists and set her jaw as if she were ready for war.

"What is it that you hate the most about your job?"

She looked up at the ceiling for a minute or two and then said, "The parents. Not all of them, but some of them treat these beautiful kids terribly. The other day I witnessed a mother picking up her daughter Tisha, who is a lovely red-haired angel. Tisha's mom smacked her twice on the bottom because she had forgotten her backpack. She told Tisha to go back and get it, and she called her a little dummy. I wanted to smack the mother, but I couldn't."

I said to Ruth, "Close your eyes, and pretend that mother is sitting in the chair across from you right now. Can you see her?" Ruth nodded. "Hear that smack again, and tell that woman what you would like to have said if you didn't have to worry about getting fired."

Ruth became very quiet, then opened one eye and looked up at me. "Can I really tell her what I would have liked to say?" I nodded, and she opened both eyes and looked at that empty chair that was now filled with that mother's presence. "You slap this precious little girl again, you bitch, and I'll slap your face so hard, you'll see stars. Don't you *ever* lay your hands on her again." Ruth's voice was strong and forceful.

I asked her to take a deep breath. "Ruth, what did the situation you witnessed remind you of?"

She really got angry then and said, "My momma used to slap me and my sister all the time for any little thing we did."

"How does that make you feel right now?"

"I'm mad as hell. She had no right to hit me or my sister."

"Ruth, pretend your mother is in that chair right now, not the mother of today, but the mother of fifteen or twenty years ago. Can you see her?"

"Yes."

"What would you like to do or say to her?"

She looked at the chair and said, "You shouldn't have slapped us. I'll never slap my children. Damn you for slapping us. We loved you so much." Ruth looked at the group, clearly in touch with her formerly buried anger. "My mother shouldn't have slapped me. I've never understood how angry that made me until now. I'm angry. I'm very angry. I know I need to do some anger release work around my mother, but if Tisha's mother ever slaps her again and I see it, I'm going to say something. At least I know now where all that rage came from."

A couple of weeks ago, Ruth wrote me a letter. She is still at the day care center. She told me that she did witness the mother hitting her little girl, but this time she was able to go over and calmly but forcefully say, "I cannot watch you hit your child. This must stop." The mother started crying and said that she knew she shouldn't hit her little girl, but she was so tired and frustrated. Ruth helped her to find a single mothers' support group. The mother is now getting the help she needs.

Ian is an excellent therapist. His practice is bursting at the seams, but what brought him to my regression workshop was his own anger. Ian admitted that he didn't know how to hold his space or deal with his clients, male or female, when they were feeling angry. Any kind of anger frightened him, he said. Sometimes when his wife displayed anger while they were talking, he even caught himself trying to change the subject.

There is an old saying: "You can only take someone as far as you've been yourself." Ian had never really probed the depths of his own anger, so he could not take his clients down into their own. He couldn't let his wife simply be angry whenever she needed to be.

"What did your father do when he was angry?" I asked.

"He yelled, screamed, and sometimes hit me and my brother and sister. I swore I'd never be like that."

"And how did your mother deal with anger?"

"She just got sick with a migraine headache or stomach problems. I think it was her way of avoiding anger entirely."

"What happened when you got angry, Ian?"

"They usually sent me to my room and told me to stay there until I could come out smiling."

In Ian's eyes, anger equaled pain. This is a very common feeling for both professionals and laypeople. I asked Ian what he did when he was angry.

He looked at the group, and then at me. Finally he said, "I don't get angry."

I said, "You don't get angry, or you don't *show* your anger?"

He thought for a moment. "I don't show it. I'm more like my mother in that sense. I have terrible stomach pain much of the time, and I think I'm developing an ulcer. I hate to admit this, but occasionally I get migraines too."

Before the seminar ended, Ian broke through the wall of terror he had constructed around his own anger and realized that being angry was all right. He did some powerful anger-release work, twisting a towel into knots, screaming at the top of his voice into a pillow, and pounding thick cushions with a tennis racquet. The whole group encouraged him, supported him, and applauded him.

After he was finished, I asked him to look around the room. "Did anyone get hurt?" I asked.

"No."

"Did you get hurt?"

"No."

"Did I get hurt?"

"No."

"See how anger doesn't always have to equal pain? The more comfortable you are with your own anger, the easier it will be for you to witness and hold the space for your wife's and your clients' anger, as long as they express it appropriately, as you did just now."

## KEEPING YOUR BODY CLEARED

If you allow yourself to consciously regress back to the times, places, and people that made you feel angry, hurt, abandoned, or disappointed, you will be able to release a lot of previously "stuffed" emotions. Once you release this grief, anger, and frustration, it will be easier for you to be present with people when they are talking about their own issues. If you don't take care of your own repressed feelings, when people bring up things that remind you of your own unfinished business, you will get triggered. At that point, you'll have few options, none of them adult. You may shut down, dissociate, disappear, or go into your head and try to deal with emotions intellectually. None of these responses are usually very satisfying to anyone.

Imagine that your body is a large, long bag. In this bag you have stuffed decades worth of hurt, sadness, anger, and tears until it weighs ten thousand pounds. You have to drag that bag around with you every day, taking it to work and into relationships with your lover, family, or friends. Sometimes the slightest slip of the tongue, the smallest put-down, or a thoughtless gesture can set you off, making you ready to run or hit others with that ten-thousand-pound bag of yours.

You need to empty that bag one pound at a time, using your body as well as your brain. Allow your tongue to say what you wanted to say twenty years ago. Scream words like "No," "Stop," "Go away," "Leave me alone," or "How could you?" Let yourself cry all the tears that you were afraid to allow anyone to see. Double up those fists and pound your bed in anger at being abandoned, forgotten, or forbidden.

Empty your body until you are only carrying about two thousand pounds of grief and rage, maybe less. Once you have done that, you will find yourself regressing less and less. Remember, unless your (or your client's) depression is biochemically induced, you (or your client) will be less depressed and you'll have more energy because you are no longer using so much energy to hold in your feelings. This will free up your energy for more creativity, loving, living, and laughing.

## REMEMBER YOUR CLIENTS AND PATIENTS ARE ALREADY REGRESSED

The single greatest thing a helping professional can do, in terms of regression, is to apply the following examples to their own lives.

## DENTISTS

The adults sitting in your dentist's chair are usually feeling about five or six years old. They are remembering the painful dental techniques they endured many years ago. No matter how far dentistry has come in developing painless procedures, they remember the old days. Give them time, some attention, and maybe a soothing touch. And for God's sake, let them shake, shiver, or cry, and be okay with that. Even encourage their expression of these feelings in some cases.

## DOCTORS, NURSES, AND OTHER MEDICAL PROFESSIONALS

Remember that most people hate hospitals, needles, and sterilized smells. Many have had needless pills, pokes, jabs, and even surgeries. Talk to them, reassure them constantly, and take your time. If you want to minimize their regression and keep them as grown up as possible, answer all their questions and give them as much information as you can. Most of all, remember what it feels like to be out of control and a patient yourself.

## POLICE

Remember that you look good to us only when we need your help. The rest of the time, your presence makes us regress back to the days of adolescence, when our parents threatened us with you. In the past, most of us committed some act that we never got caught doing, and now forty years later, when you pull up behind us, we are sure we have finally been found out. Also remember that we have seen hundreds of hours of bad television depicting corrupt and brutal cops bashing in heads just for fun. Talk to the people you pull over in a soothing, nonaggressive tone of voice. Remember that we are afraid of you. Don't always interpret our fear as guilt or hostility toward you or what you represent.

## THERAPISTS, COUNSELORS, SOCIAL WORKERS

Remember that, until recently, most Americans thought seeing a therapist meant that they were crazy. Therapy was only for schizophrenics and lunatics. Clients or patients may associate seeing you with being two steps away from a mental hospital. Deep down inside, most people who see you feel they are somehow defective, broken, or bad and need fixing. This feeling sends them into a major regression. You can minimize the regression by reassuring them right from the start that what they are doing is a healthy thing and not something to be ashamed of. And remember that you can only take your patients as far as you have gone yourself.

## HOW TO REDUCE REGRESSION IN CLIENTS

One of the single greatest causes of regression in patients is the psychological phenomenon of transference. Freud and others more qualified than I have written extensively on this subject. What they did not write about, however, is the techniques that can spare you a great deal of miscommunication and misunderstanding and speed up the process of bonding with your client.

This is an exercise I do at the beginning of all of my individual client sessions and at all of my seminars and retreats. I ask everyone to close their eyes and then open them, look at me, and see if I remind them of anyone from their past. Hands shoot up and out come the words *father, uncle, ex-boyfriend, ex-husband* or *wife, mother, sister, coach,* or *teacher.* I then ask them to take a piece of paper and write down all the ways that I am not like those people, including my appearance, style of dress, speech, and what they know about my background. I then ask them to make a list of the ways that I remind them of those people, and then to compare the lists. The second list usually has only one or two items on it, while the first list usually has at least a dozen, sometimes more. Somehow this exercise tends to keep us all in the present and allows me to build a place of safety where we can experience Conscious Regression around the issues they brought to the workshop, instead of wasting valuable time fending off unnecessary and unintentional transference.

## SAFETY—THE KEY TO MINIMIZING REGRESSION

After I do the exercise to avoid transference, I begin to deepen the safety that my workshop participants and individual clients feel. I reassure them that everything said in the private session or group will be confidential, and I ask everyone to agree to this. The second thing I tell them is that every exercise or task is completely voluntary—nothing is mandatory. They do not even have to stay in the room. If they feel they need air or space, one of my assistants will follow them out of the room and calmly check in with them to see if they want to be alone or if they would like to talk.

A big part of creating safety, and thus minimizing Trance Regression, is setting up the rule that there will be no interrupting the person who is talking, and no confrontation on the group's part, should something that someone says throw them into a regression. I encourage witnessing participants to contain their own feelings until we can give them the appropriate time and attention to deal with the issues that came up for them.

## A LITTLE TRICK OF THE TRADE

If one of my participants misconstrues something I said or did, becoming extremely upset, nervous, anxious, scared, or angry, I ask them to take one of my assistants aside and tell them what is going on. I call this the Detour Method (see pages 180–190). Afterward, if they still feel they need to talk to me, I'll be happy to take the time to do so. Ninety-nine times out of a hundred, they will see that what I said or didn't say, or did or didn't do, was more about their own history than about me.

The second part of the trick should really be called "How to keep arrows out of a workshop facilitator." I do it whenever someone comes up to me and says, "I really need to talk to you about something that went on in the last session."

I always take a deep breath and say, "You know, I really need to rest now. If we talked about this now, I wouldn't be able to give you the clear hearing and attention you may need. Let's talk this evening after dinner."

If they say, "Sure, that will be fine. I can wait," their ability to contain their feelings is a clear signal to me that they are not regressed but in the present. Then I will say, "You know what, let's just go ahead and talk about this now." Most of the time, what they have to say will only require about five minutes, during which I can listen and perhaps make an apology.

But if they say their issue can't wait until after dinner, then I set a firm boundary. I tell them that they must wait at least until I'm more rested. Then they will be less likely to regress when we do speak.

## TELLING YOUR CLIENTS OR FRIENDS WHERE YOU ARE AT

This brings me to a subject that will make many therapists and counselors cringe. One way to keep yourself and your clients from regressing is to honestly admit to them how you are feeling at the moment. This goes against the grain of nearly all schools of psychology and psychotherapy. Only a few therapists have dared to consider the value of admitting to their current emotional states. The great psychologist Sidney Jourard wrote a very important book on the therapist's need, and indeed his duty, to disclose certain information to his clients. This book, which is still in print, is titled *The Transparent Self*. Most of Jourard's peers thought he was flagrantly disobeying the therapist's code of "We're here to talk about your problems, not mine." The only place that would employ him was a Florida university that taught nursing. Basically what Jourard said was that if you are not willing to tell your clients something about who you are and the struggles you are facing, then why should they trust you with their private pain?

Now don't misunderstand me. I'm not suggesting that you tell your clients about your bad marriage or the amount you lost trading stock. If my client comes in and says, "How are you today?" I might say, "I'm a little tired" or "I'm sad"—in other words, the truth.

If they then say, "Really? Tell me about it. Maybe I can help," I say, "No, thank you. I have a therapist or friend I'll be speaking with later. Let's look at what's going on with you today."

If I'm in such pain that I cannot maintain my maturity and adult objectivity, then I think I should say so. The day after I broke up with a woman whom I loved very dearly, I had to go and do a four-day Facing the Fire Intensive. I told the participants and my assistants that I wasn't in great shape emotionally. As it turned out, I came up with the idea of having my assistant help me to consciously regress in front of the participants. I found myself going back to my earlier wounding, when my mother emotionally abandoned me. I got some deep release work out of that experience and afterward felt much lighter. I was then able to proceed with the workshop in an emotionally present state. I don't have to do this very often, and I wouldn't suggest that therapists reveal everything about themselves. But if you are with a client and you are feeling sad, angry, and lonely, and they ask you, "Are you okay?" you should answer truthfully. If you say, "Oh yes, I'm fine" and you really are not, the average client will immediately see the incongruity between your words and your true emotional state. This will, at worst, make them regress back to some other time when people lied to them or did not tell them the whole truth; at best, it will make for a crummy session.

If I am less than authentic about how I am feeling, why should I expect another person to be authentic? In a workshop, if I ask a participant to do something or try something experientially that I have not done myself, then I will do it with them. So if they are going to feel embarrassed, I'll be feeling the same.

Again, let me say that this concept goes against what we have commonly been taught in our training programs. But just because an approach is standard does not necessarily mean that it is correct or healthy. For instance, if I'm nervous before giving a public talk, the first thing I do is to tell my audience that I'm nervous. This always makes me feel less nervous, enabling me to proceed more easily with my talk. The audience, who are mostly scared to death of public speaking themselves, can then empathize, allowing me to grow back up and give the talk. Toastmasters, the most successful school of public speaking, says to never, never tell your audience that you are afraid, because this will belie your credibility. But my own experience has not borne out this dogma.

## CREATING CONSCIOUS COMMUNITY

Many therapists, doctors, lawyers, and other helping professionals have groups where they can laugh, tell jokes, share a drink, discuss a case, or go fishing. But few have a community to whom they can turn during stressful, difficult times and to whom they can express all of their emotions without feeling guilty, embarrassed, shamed, or belittled. So when it is not appropriate to tell a client or a group how I'm feeling, I turn to a safe, supportive group of friends and colleagues with whom I can share those feelings. I can call them when I'm feeling small, or visit them and get the attention, empathy, time, touch, and release that I need. Sometimes I may need to contact one or more of these people before I give my next workshop or have that deep discussion with my wife.

Sixteen years ago, Dan Jones and I created our own conscious community, which we call PEER (Primary, Emotional, Energy, Recovery). We set up this network so that if we were going through difficult times, we could talk with one another and recover the energy that had been sapped by a person or experience, restabilizing ourselves emotionally. This worked so well for us that we began teaching this process to therapists and laypeople. To date, the PEER Community has grown to about ten thousand members, all of whom have participated in some level of this training and have formed their own leaderless support groups around the country. We receive no monetary benefits from their doing so. All of these people have each other's phone numbers, and they set up special meeting times to get together and share their tears, laughter, anger, frustration, and joy. They also share new techniques to help people release their pent-up emotions in a healthy and positive manner.

The question for helping professionals is a simple one: Do you have an adequate number of people who can support you, especially since you have made the choice to be a professional helper? If not, then why not? I have been going to twelve-step meetings for years. On more than a few occasions, I have asked those therapists who have trained with me if they find these meetings as useful as I do. I'm surprised that most think they are useful but rarely attend themselves. They are afraid they might see a client there and feel overly exposed. I can appreciate these feelings, but I have had to make them secondary to my own need to be heard, seen, and listened to when I cannot find a member of my personal support community to help me grow back up when I regress.

My suggestion is to find five to seven people who will not shame you, demean you, or belittle you when you share your feelings with them. Hopefully, you and they can use this book for some guidance to create a supportive community. This community should be woven together like a strong net so that when you run, fly, succeed, fail, or fall, caring people will be there to catch you and nurture you until you feel all grown up again. At other times, when others do the same, you can be part of the net that catches them.

I hope this material has helped someone somewhere. If it has, please pass along what I've said. Know that regression can be a gift from God, and that this material and the writing of this book was God's gift to me.

# SUGGESTED READING

## ACADEMIC AND SCHOLARLY TEXTS

Balint, Michael. *The Basic Fault: Therapeutic Aspects of Regression.* Evanston, IL: Northwestern University Press, 1964.

Jackson, Helene, ed. *Using Self Psychology in Psychotherapy.* London: Jason Aronson, 1994.

Kramer, Selma, M.D., and Salman Akhtar, M.D. *Mahler and Kohut: Perspectives on Development, Psychopathology, and Technique.* London: Jason Aronson, 1994.

Masterson, James F., M.D. *The Real Self: A Developmental, Self, and Object Relations Approach.* New York: Brunner/Mazel Publishers, 1985.

Seinfeld, Jeffrey, M.D. *Containing Rage, Terror, and Despair: An Object Relations Approach to Psychotherapy.* London: Jason Aronson, 1996.

———. *Interpreting and Holding: The Paternal and Maternal Functions of the Psychotherapist.* London: Jason Aronson, 1993.

White, Marjorie T., and Marcella B. Weiner. *The Theory and Practice of Self Psychology.* New York: Brunner/Mazel Publishers, 1986.

Winnicott, D.W. *Home Is Where We Start From: Essays by a Psychoanalyst.* New York: W.W. Norton & Co., 1986.

Wolf, Ernest S., M.D. *Treating the Self: Elements of Clinical Self Psychology.* New York: Guilford Press, 1988.

## PERSONAL GROWTH PSYCHOLOGY

Allen, Patricia, Ph.D. *Getting to "I Do": The Secret to Doing Relationships Right.* New York: Avon Books, 1994.

Caldwell, Christine, Ph.D., ed. *Getting in Touch: The Guide to New Body-Centered Therapies.* Wheaton, IL: Quest Books, 1997.

Grinder, John, and Richard Bandler. *Trance-Formations: Neuro-Linguistic Programming and the Structure of Hypnosis.* Moab, UT: Real People Press, 1981.

Jackins, Harvey. *The Human Situation.* Seattle: Rational Island Publishers, 1973.

Lee, John. *Facing the Fire: Experiencing and Expressing Anger Appropriately.* New York: Bantam, 1993.

Levine, Peter A. *Waking the Tiger: Healing Trauma.* Berkeley, CA: North Atlantic Books, 1997.

Montagu, Ashley. *Touching: The Human Significance of the Skin.* New York: Perennial Library, 1971.

Nelson, Jane, Ed.D., Cheryl Erwin, M.A., and Roslyn Duffy. *Positive Discipline: The First Three Years.* Roseville, CA: Prima Publishing, 1998.

Pert, Candace B., Ph.D. *Molecules of Emotion: Why You Feel the Way You Feel.* New York: Scribner, 1997.

Robbins, Ronald. *Rythmic Integration: Finding Wholeness in the Cycle of Change.* New York: Pulse, 1990.

Sapolsky, Robert M. *Why Zebras Don't Get Ulcers: An Updated Guide to Stress, Stress-Related Diseases, and Coping.* New York: W.H. Freeman & Co., 1994.

Thomas, Sandra, Ph.D., and Cheryl Jefferson. *Use Your Anger: A Woman's Guide to Empowerment.* New York: Pocket Books, 1996.

Wolinsky, Stephen, Ph.D. *Trances People Live: Healing Approaches in Quantum Psychology.* Hartford, CT.: Bramble Co., 1991.

# OTHER RESOURCES

For a complete list of my schedules, workshops, seminars, and trainings, please contact me at 201 Brentwood Court, Woodstock, GA 30188. Or you can call toll free at 1-888-800-2099 or 678-494-5011.

For biography, testimonials, live chat, or schedules, visit the Web site *www.flyingboy.com.*

You can e-mail me at *theflyingboy@aol.com* or fax inquiries to me at 678-494-6878.

To order books and tapes, you can e-mail me at *fbordering@aol.com* or fax your orders to 678-494-6878.

# INDEX